You're Crazy

You're Crazy

First-hand accounts of Mental Health Struggle, Addiction, and Trauma from the Punk Scene

Editor Craig Lewis

Better Days Recovery Press

You're Crazy Volume 1 © 2013 Craig Lewis and the individual contributors

Revised 09/14.

Edited by Renee Mandrake
Layout by Jonathan Rowland
Cover design and sheep by Jennifer C. McMahon • "You are not a black sheep." jenniferchristinemcmahon@gmail.com

ISBN: 978-1-304-59280-4

Better Days Recovery Press
yourecrazycontact@gmail.com

http://www.betterdaysrecovery.com/
http://www.punksinrecovery.com/

Contents

"You are not alone. We all have our scars, our crazy hair, our tattoos and emotional marks. Don't let the flock fool you."
   —Jen McMahon

I would like to express my heartfelt thanks to the following people who helped support and create this book. Jonathan Rowland for his invaluable editing and layout work. Jennifer McMahon for her beautiful cover design. Patrick Clement, Damian "the Samhain Kid" Saiz, Carrie L. Keeler, and Christina for their editorial support. Laura Kaplan for her editing assistance. Jimmy Murphy for his legal support and guidance. All of you have committed your time, effort, and hard work toward the completion of this book and without all of you this book would not exist. Finally, I would like to thank Michelle Watson for all of her emotional support that has helped me see this project through to its completion.

Craig Lewis
December 21, 2013

Introduction

Craig Lewis

You're Crazy! I have been told this over and over again throughout my life. These two words have done as much damage to me as any punch or kick ever has. I have lived a life of chronic mental health struggle, trauma, substance use, and dysfunction. I have been called crazy countless times. People have said this about me, that I am crazy, to invalidate me and my life experience. Calling me crazy has always been an effective way to devalue me; but those words no longer hold this power.

I think it is important to explain why it has hurt so much when I've been called "crazy." It is also important to share the self-hatred I felt when people would describe me as "crazy" instead of trying to understand where I was coming from. I desperately needed those around me to consider that my reaction to an upsetting situation was often a reasonable reaction to an unreasonable situation or circumstance. Even as my reactions may have been extreme or outrageous; there were explanations behind my behavior and I was not, nor ever was "crazy." People would say this about me instead of considering the facts of the situation and the constant repetition, with which I experienced this, every time, cut me like a knife.

I have been listening to punk rock and hardcore since 1988 when I was fourteen and metal for years earlier. I've considered myself a punk rocker almost as long. I met my first punk rocker during my first experience as an inpatient at a mental hospital. Meeting this woman and her influence on me by making punk rock something that I could connect and belong to has long been one of the only things that kept me alive as I experienced endless years of hell and trauma throughout my life.

Being a part of the punk scene has been and still is an amazing experience for me. I have met some wonderful and incredible people over the years. The punk scene was and in many ways still is, a place where people like me, rebellious and troubled youth, could find a safe haven from the trappings of the conformist society surrounding us. This provided a lot of opportunities for us to be the unique individuals we are. However, there was also a price to pay.

As someone who has struggled with a mental health condition my entire life, being in the punk scene allowed me to live a reckless, unhealthy, and self-destructive life with little to no objection or guidance toward living a healthier life. I got high for over ten years and I surrounded myself with people who did drugs so I had more access to getting high. Getting high everyday was not a good way for me to manage my mental health struggles yet it allowed for me to be social, which was crucial for me.

So I had the idea to create a fanzine that would include stories of my peers in the punk scene who have struggled in ways similar to me. I put out the call via the internet and received many submissions. It took me a long time to get the book in gear due to my own mental health and life struggles getting in the way and I apologize to everyone who has had to wait for me to finally get the book published. I was fortunate to have several friends who helped with editing the stories. It was up to each writer if they wanted to take the suggestions of the editors or not, outside of grammar issues, etc. Each writer provided written permission for their stories to be included in this book. Finally, after two years of working on the book, I got it into high gear. I found a supportive editor friend who has helped put the book together and a wonderful artist for the cover. This has been a long and tough process. However, if you are reading this introduction, you know that we all succeeded. There will be subsequent volumes of *You're Crazy*. If you are interested in telling your story in a future volume, please get in contact.

One reason that I wanted to compile first-hand accounts of people from the punk scene who live with mental health struggles, addictions, and/or trauma was to help give a voice to people who have been misunderstood and stigmatized. In my experience in the punk scene—a safe place for me to be dysfunctional—I was misunderstood. My living habits were that of a sick person yet I was nurtured to continue this way of life, which had an immensely detrimental impact on my wellness, happiness, and stability. Many people living in similarly rough ways surrounded me. Yet as the years passed on, many of these people got their lives in order while my life stagnated. I desperately needed to be nurtured toward wellness during these years. Unfortunately I received little support toward getting well. This is something that I feel must be addressed for others as well.

Another reason why I compiled these first-hand accounts was so that the writers could tell their stories to their peers in order to be better understood. I want the writers to feel liberated and empowered and by sharing their stories here; no longer simply classified as "crazy" or some other invalidating word. I also want the people reading these stories to be our allies in destroying the stigma that we all face in society. I want our community to become more supportive and helpful of each other. I want "my people" to suffer less and be happy, healthy, and well. For anyone reading these stories who does not have lived experience as a punk rocker; I welcome you to learn more about our world. We are your sons, daughters, neighbors, friends, students, teachers, clients, and the list goes on.

I want "my people" to know that we can learn to live happier and healthier lives. I want "my people" to know that we can be punk rockers and we can also take care of ourselves and find proactive and helpful ways of managing our mental health, substance use, and trauma issues. I want "my people" to know that we don't have to be stuck suffering; that things can be better and that we can support each other in creating better lives for ourselves.

Many of us have lost people we care about to suicide. Many of us have lost friends to addiction. Many of us have lost friends due to reckless living. I want this book to show that it is possible to make things better. Each story in this book is the real deal, from the heart and honest. It is not easy to talk about our struggles yet it is incredibly powerful for us to be sharing our stories. We get better by talking about what we experience. We must not live in shame and we must not live in silence. We must empower ourselves and our peers to live happier and healthier lives. We are not crazy! We are unique and worthy individuals and we deserve to be understood. When you know our story you can understand us better. We have value as human beings and as punk rockers. We are bold and often very loud and proud. Let us no longer remain silent! Let us rise up and create a community of wellness!

For you, for me, and for all of us.

Bringing Awkward Back

Antonia Tsangaris

'm bringing awkward back and that has to be ok with you, because it's taken too long for it to be ok with me. That fight gets tiring.

It shouldn't be anyone's responsibility to constantly assert themselves just to exist. That's what it's like sometimes, this world's got the volume turned up to eleven, which can have its time and place, but hot damn, turning it to three, four, or five is good too.

No one wants to be That Guy, the one who actually speaks up and kills the party because a bunch of extroverts decided they have a monopoly on society's volume knob.

Well guess what y'all, I am That Guy.

This is what That Guy looks like.

This is what That Guy likes to do, and this is what That Guy thinks about when you're not around (and sometimes when you are).

While this girl is the only That Guy this girl feels comfortable speaking for, I know for certain I'm not alone.

I have to ask, where are you, That Guys? That's the big paradox of bringing awkward back. As much as we need to crawl back to the fortress of solitude just to stay "sane" and "happy" in this world turned up to eleven, no one thrives in isolation. We need water and sunlight too, delicate flowers that we are, probably more so than the cacti of the world who have it much easier.

That's why I'm bringing awkward back, because sometimes it isn't safe for us to leave the fortress of solitude when there's kryptonite like small talk, eye contact, fourty-hour workweeks, long-term cohabitative monogamous relationships and the meeting with the show and the after-party of the after-party of the after-party lurking around every corner. Not only am I tired of not feeling safe, I'm tired of not getting to meet, know and love my siblings-in-arms because they don't feel safe enough to experience that.

That's what this really is y'all, a call-to-arms. I'm asking for nothing less than revolution. This requires self-organization of the That Guys, on our terms, for the sake of taking back the current social paradigms, creating new ones that actually resonate with our needs and experiences, without infringing on the autonomy, agency and basic comfort of normal[1] people. Especially our well intentioned intimates, confidants and allies.

So, I'm bringing awkward back, good for me. But what does that mean for you, O well-intentioned flower of a less delicate disposition than myself? It means checking it and not getting sketched out, offended or haughty when I can't make direct eye contact for that long.

I know they're the windows to the soul and such and if I'm up for it, I just might take a peek. Maybe the part of your soul that shines through the rest of you is so interesting and intoxicating that I barely need your eyes to know how great you are and share this moment with you.

Yeah, you've got some pretty eyes and in theory I'd love to spend all day getting lost in them, but in practice it just takes a peek or two to know you're still there, still full of more magic than I could ever hope to fathom (but can't wait to figure out how). Any more than that would be overdosing on a wonderful drug that just might kill me in a quantity that large. How romantic is that shit?

---

1 Wherever this word comes up, please replace "normal" with whatever term you feel best describes people who don't experience what you do (sane, neuro-typical, enabled, etc.) I just needed something concise.

Sometimes it'll seem like your soul's got nothing going on and there's no point in looking there anyway. But, as anyone who's bothered to look into my soul a little can confirm, I'll assume the best in people unless they give me a reason not to, and I stay focused on the people who don't.

Now small talk, what the fuck is up with small talk? I don't know what that stuff means and I'm in no real hurry to learn.

Fuck it y'all, I want BIG talk. Who says you need to know someone's name, where they're from and what they do for a living in order to share your favorite spot to watch the sunset, or your uncle's French toast recipe, or the details of your abuse histories?

Fucking get to the heart of the matter, you know? Because as much as I'm advocating bringing awkward back and creating spaces for those of us who can't be conventionally social all the time, I'll be damned if we don't build walls between each other that don't need to be there.

We've been taught it's not safe to trust your neighbor just because a few douche-clowns ruined it for the rest of us. Damn if I don't fall for that far too often.

It really fucking scares me to think that this community we keep talking about building, that sometimes seems to center around getting crunk with each other for hours on end, might not be all that much safer for me than the dominant culture.

As much as we desperately need safe spaces to be alone AND make human connections in ways that actually speak to our needs and experiences; as much as we all need to bring awkward back, we need to learn to get REAL with each other. That means going past the small talk, until it starts to actually mean something.

It means talking about what you think no one understands or even wants to hear because it's important to you and part of your reality; like how really fucking awkward you are and how you're sick of that being a liability.

I'll be damned if these words might not be exactly what someone needs to hear. Maybe it will even be the gentle poke in the right direction to start shaking off years of internalized negativity. Or to figure out how to live outside the fortress of solitude without getting ripped to shreds, and start building social connections that are actually meaningful, instead of ones that the dominant culture says you should have.

On that note, please don't call me shy without my explicit prior consent.

Call me "socially cautious" if you must but I am not necessarily shy. I am one of the bravest people I know, so is everyone else who's even attempting to stay alive and present in a world that would rather ignore them completely.

If I was shy this would never have left my notebook and I'm proud to admit I wrote it with an audience in mind.

That in itself might be awkward but that's something I want to undo; the idea that because I can't or don't relate to people the way we're taught we're supposed to I shouldn't bother in the first place. God forbid I offend someone or create one of those dreaded (you guessed it) awkward moments.

I really wish it didn't have to be this way. I don't doubt I've offended or at least confused some well-intentioned normal people and maybe even fellow introverts, awkward kids and/or delicate flowers lower on that spectrum than myself. If you are offended by this, really stop, sit back and think about why.

If I've said anything completely off-base and horrible I'd appreciate a respectful callout. That's part of getting real with each other.

Ideally our personal boundaries should never be violated or even pushed too severely outside of consensual contexts. It's a great idea to examine where those boundaries came from, why they're there in the first place and if they're really all that necessary or beneficial.

I think if I say too much more here I'll slip into my old habit of apologizing for sharing whatever's on my awkward little mind and somewhat weaken the whole point of how I'm tired of apologizing for being "different."

So yeah, I'm awkward and loving it. Hopefully you are too.

Hard Traveling

Bambi Bailey

'm not going to use words like mental illness and addiction here, I'm just going to talk a little bit about my travels as a dirty kid (I'm not a fan of the word "gutter punk," but if that's what works for you, that's fine), and the stupid shit I did, the mistakes I made, and if it helps anyone at all to either recognize some of the same things that are going on in their own life, or helps anyone to be able to not make those same mistakes, then so much the better.

Traveling was vaguely similar to what it was like being a drunken teenager in Boston, except the punk rockers were smellier, the drugs were harder, and the blunders had bigger consequences. It is not always easy being a girl on the street. When you are young and stupid it becomes really easy to start judging yourself according to how appealing you are to the males around you. For a long fucking time I truly believed that my value as a person was directly related to what was between my legs, to how much or how little I was wanted by guys. Naturally, this mindset did not often lead me down wise paths.

The very first guy that expressed any interest in me whatsoever became my boyfriend. He started hitting me three weeks into our "relationship," only when he was drunk, and never anywhere that other people could see the bruises. It took no time at all for me to accept this as just the way it was; I had no trust in myself as a capable person at all, I didn't believe that I could go it alone and so I stayed with a total piece of shit instead of kicking him to the curb and moving on. Even when, after two months and 3,000 miles, he date-raped me in an empty squat in Hollywood, I didn't leave him. I really thought that I had nowhere at all to go, no action to take against him (which is *never* true; I could have found a drop-in center, or gone to a hospital, or sucked it up and phoned someone-*anyone*, or even-dare I say it-called the police on the sonofabitch. I could have done a lot of things, and I didn't). But it took him slipping up, and other people noticing for me to actually leave him; he punched me in the stomach in someone else's van one night for having the audacity to suggest that there was not enough space between the two front seats for both of us to sleep on the floor. The next day the other two people living in the van told me that I should leave him and ride with them. They gave me an option, and I took it.

Things got a little more complicated with the next relationship, especially once the drugs took over both our lives. I got pregnant in Virginia, and found out about it in Florida two days after a week-long crack bender. They don't tell you that when you get a pregnancy test you will automatically be drug tested also. The crack didn't show up, but a weeks-previous toke of weed did, so I got a lecture anyway. A month later I had an abortion. I don't think my boyfriend ever really forgave me for it, he ditched me in Wisconsin in February to get strung out and then skip town for the northwest. It sounds so stupid now, but at the time I wanted to understand why something like heroin could possibly be so much more important to him than me. That was why I bought the first bag.

But it was in California that I actually came to understand a few things, when I had been using for long enough to start experiencing dope-sickness. Hitch-hiking from Berkeley to Portland, Oregon on the 101 was arduous going. It took six days to make the trip and I had no idea why I could not sleep at night, why my sleeping bag darkened with sweat so quickly, why I tossed and turned and twitched until morning . . . nothing made sense until we got to Yreka, and stumbled upon a boy who had a crush on my friend, as well as a single syringe and a phone number. I got "well" for the first time that day, felt the lead drain out of my body after the shot, realized I hadn't just missed the feeling, I'd needed it.

Seattle was, in retrospect, a foolish place to go, but I was back with my boyfriend, I would have followed him anywhere. He was three weeks clean when we got there, and I'd been clean ten days. A girl approached him in Reservoir Park not ten minutes after we'd thrown our gear onto a bench and thanked our ride. He walked away with her and left me with our bags—like a chump—returning thirty minutes later with a shot for each of us. We stayed there six months; observed with dull eyes the chaos of emotion that burst out of America after September 11, lost so much weight we were little more than skeletons and skin, hated each other but couldn't ever stick with breaking up—bound by our shared miseries, lied, scammed, and stole from anyone who turned their back long enough for us to get away with it, we circled the drain on Broadway Street, barely human. We escaped on a bus, muscling black tar heroin in the Greyhound bathroom and shivering under our blankets for five days, Washington State all the way back to Boston. Word had already gotten back to the East Coast about my vices. I saw Arriel and Nathan at a table outside Au Bon Pain in Harvard Square and got The Lecture; dope is bad, don't do it. All I could do was hang my head and nod while thinking spitefully, you're going to relapse too, you hypocrite. I love Arriel, but I felt indignant and self-righteous when she talked to me that way, regardless of her good intentions and the caring place her words came from. I was clean, wasn't I? What more did she want?

I thought I had gotten smarter, dabbling with heroin while working on a farm in Virginia from October 2001 until February 2002, but never using for more than two days in a row. Toby overdosed in a housing project in Baltimore in January, people stood around and laughed, "it's a dead whitey," while we dragged him to my car. He didn't die, although he should've. It took seven hours for us to get him to a hospital back in Virginia. I started boxing up our things that night, preparing to leave. We went south, smoked some crack in Savannah, both got arrested in New Orleans, then turned north to Madison when I was released. My boyfriend was arrested the second day we were there, and I turned into a wreck (it was my drunken hollering that got the cops called). A friend of a friend gave me half a bag to calm me down. I didn't put the needle down again for almost a year. Sucked right back into it, just like that.

The events that would ultimately put the idea of "getting my shit together" occurred in 2005—although it would take years longer than that to start feeling like a whole person again; my father passed away after a long struggle with Alzheimer's in April and Arriel died in Boston two months later, of an overdose. I attended both memorials, got strung out again . . . .and then Hurricane Katrina happened while I was working at Ocean Spray in Cape Cod, numbing all emotion with dope inside a soggy tent. I quit work, left with a friend, kicked in my car while she drove, arrived in New Orleans clean on Thanksgiving day. Louisiana changed everything.

People cared, and without ulterior motives—fuck-ups and junkies can smell ulterior motives from miles away. A friend in Lafayette convinced me to apply to the local university, and I got in. Seven years after high school I went back to school. If there hadn't been positive, encouraging people around it never would have happened. From the outside looking in, being on the streets may look so horrible there's no way to imagine anyone in their right mind staying homeless, but when it's the only thing you know, the only terrain you know how to navigate, and every effort to escape it turns into another runaround, wild goose chase, or dead end—it can be easy enough to get stuck there. Getting out is the hard part.

A lot of things went right in my case, I was lucky enough to have an opportunity available to me when I started over; couches to sleep on, food to eat, some inheritance money to put deposit down on an apartment—it is nowhere near that easy for everyone. But personal, human support is maybe the most important aid that anyone can give to someone who is trying to improve their life. Whether it's getting off drugs, or quitting drinking, or getting housing, or mental health assistance, or going back to school . . . the people who stay with you during the struggle upward are the best in the world. There's always plenty of other bodies around at the bottom, people who think the mess is fun, or who can't stand being miserable alone, or get off on the self-destruction of others—those people are a dime a dozen. There will be less people who help you stand up afterward, but they exist. If we can all figure out who those people are in our lives, and try helping them to evolve just like they help us, then we will be doing good work in the world.

My Life With Depression

Ben Smart

Although I've only been aware of my mental illnesses for roughly five years, they have been affecting my life for as long as I can remember. I suffer from depression as well as general anxiety disorder, of which I experience the detrimental effects of each and every day. Before my political stances, before my ethical stances, before I encounter the world in any of the various roles I fulfill or as any facet of my own identity, I first take in my life through a lens created by the irrationality of my illnesses. For the past five years I've become increasingly aware of these diseases, their symptoms, and their effects. Every year I have better understood their impact on my entire life. I've learned my own personal methods for coping and growing beyond their limitations, which are sometimes simply trading one kind of damaging behavior for another. My efforts to remain challenging myself, to keep improving the quality of my life and exploring my own limitations due to these disorders, have been the most frustrating, confusing, emotional, difficult, and (quite honestly) terrifying struggles I have ever pulled through and will continue to undertake.

My first encounters with depression and anxiety go back to my early childhood. I almost definitely inherited these traits from my mother's family. My aunt on this side is a recovered alcoholic, another has voluntarily fled the family and lives with addiction to various substances, and an uncle became a suicide victim shortly after I was born. My predisposition was combined by a series of traumatic events in my family life, religious life in the Catholic church, and my suffering social life in a small, conservative New England town. Not having realized my experiences and details of my life were not "normal" and under the belief I was experiencing a "rough patch" that would magically end upon fleeing this town, I never considered seeking help or counseling. I became excellent at hiding my emotions from my family, and because I excelled in school, displayed no outward symptoms, or otherwise gave reasons for the adults around me to force me to seek help.

It took the completion of a two-year college degree, the closing of my school, the dispersion of my only close friends, the pressures transitioning into a new city and new college where I knew nobody, as well as tension and conflict within my family, to get myself finally into a meeting with my school's counselor and subsequently into therapy. This also only after being suggested by a friend. Luckily I am a very strong, stubborn person with a strong survival instinct: all of the three professionals I have ever met with were all shocked to hear my stories and that I had not ended up as another teenage suicide in a small town.

Having grown up in a former factory town of a population under 5,000 and a graduating class around eighty-five, it's needless to say there was nothing resembling a radical or punk community in town, or nearby. My first experiences with somewhat non-mainstream punk music happened when I was twelve or thirteen (I was given a Vans *Off the Wall* sampler CD at a ski/skate shop by an employee), although I grew up only 100 miles north of Boston, had no car among myself or my friends, parents who were not interested in driving to the city out of necessity (let alone to take me to a show), and absolutely no money that wasn't spent on new skateboards, shoes, or the occasional CD. Rather than being indoctrinated into the subculture via those already active, or being handed a flyer or a 'zine, or from peer influence, I was stuck with my own limited means.

My education of punk was limited to what I could procure from peer-to-peer networks, DIY Geocities pages of punk flyers, stories, and the occasional downloadable recordings. I hadn't any exposure to any contemporary scene, minus a friend who was obsessed with *Boston Beatdown* videos and gave me my first (ill-informed) impression on what "hardcore" was about. Punk, according to the limited sources I had, seemed to always be in the past-tense, since all I seemed to keep finding were historical materials. I had almost no close friendships and lacked a supporting network of other peers that could have been supplied by having access to a radical or punk community like the one I would later discover for myself in Boston.

Transferring schools and moving into the city marked a large change in my life. This transition spurred on a period of growth and self-improvement, not just through therapy, but also through the meeting of new friends, forming of richer relationships, and positive peer influence. Early success with my psychiatrist coincided with meeting a new and more diverse network of creatives, and then becoming indoctrinated into the Boston hardcore punk scene.

At the time when I had moved to Boston, a few friends were facilitating metal, punk, and mixed bill shows in our school's main building. Attending these got me excited about attending DIY shows in basements and alternative spaces all over town, and the right flyers and the right contacts to achieve access to them. Although I am extremely critical of hardcore and punk as a social movement or subculture, I can personally attest that DIY events are a crucial means of meeting some of the most amazing, supportive, intelligent, ethically upright people you may ever meet. If it weren't for the meeting of other like-minded people, and through their support, I doubt I'd be as confident or well-developed a person I am today. I was fortunate enough to share a work study job with someone who was already established in a certain circle of vegan, straight edge punks that now serves as my social base, and has for years.

Between consistent and constructive therapy sessions, supportive schools in the punk and artistic community, and success with antidepressants, I was experiencing remarkable changes. Within a year and a half of moving to Boston I had gone vegan and sobered up (although I had only drank for just over two years I realized I had abused the substance, using it as a crutch, an escape from my emotions, as well as discovered a correlation between drinking and onset depression and anxiety attacks). I was slowly but surely learning methods of over-coming my illnesses and undoing the damage and social condition-ing pressed upon me in my upbringing. Upon finishing my degree, I decided to stay in Boston, where I still live. Although my health insur-ance benefits (and subsequently, my access to antidepressants) end-ed shortly after graduating I've actually managed to keep challenging myself to learn new methods and ways to keep growing, improving, and combating my illnesses.

One of the most important realizations I've had in the two years or so since without therapy or medication is that staying mentally healthy is an incredible act of defiance as our healthcare industry is developed to create profits rather than a healthy populace throughout our entire society. I've had inexpensive state health insurance with great mental health benefits that have been pretty easy to acquire, keep, and utilize for doctor appointments and emergencies. Unfortunately, I discov-ered last year during a sustained major depressive episode that few, if any providers accept my insurance due to the low payout they receive. Despite the lack of treatment, I've still managed to do better than "just getting by." My partner, Brittney, has been incredibly understanding and helpful during the past eight months. My friends have always been concerned and supportive and continue to be so. While I still expe-rience low serotonin production, and though I remove myself from situations where full blown anxiety attacks are triggered, I still expe-rience intense anxiety several times a month and in lower amounts at least many times a week. My cognition seems to gradually improve, though, as I've become more and more aware of these thought pro-cesses and much better able to talk about my own experiences much more clearly and accurately with those who I feel comfortable talking to, and are also comfortable listening. Somehow, despite stacked odds against me, I've been able to survive twenty-seven years of mental ill-ness. I've been able to develop an amazing awareness of who I am, the diseases I cope with, a support network, and hopefully a lifetime of continual growth.

Living with mental illness, to me, is a major responsibility that lacks positive models in our culture. With the thick amounts of stig-ma surrounding mental health in mainstream society, the lack of dia-logue surrounding it in hardcore punk/radical culture has allowed this stigma to remain pervasive. While 'zines, blogs, workshops, benefit shows, fests, and other forms have emerged within these communities and allow for the discussion of other equally (or more) intense subject matter (to name a few: LGBTQ issues, women's rights, racism and prejudice, rape culture, systematic violence, and oppression) to one extent or another, mental health is a topic that has remained mostly untouched despite its urgency. I have tried to be more and more open about my own experiences, and even with this personal mission I still find it incredibly difficult to talk about my experiences, even with those closest to me, due to feelings triggered by this stigma. The lack of voices speaking out against this stigma, and others like it, is a silent widespread agreement that affirms its existence and maintains a cultural pressure to keep quiet (in regards to mental health and other stigmatized personal experiences) and stay ashamed.

I've felt this pressure repeatedly throughout my life. Through my mother's side of the family I learned the importance of keeping secrets to keep up appearances and suppress scandals. I learned through my exposure to Catholic dogma for seventeen years to feel bad about myself, that everything happens due to God's design, and that all things happen for a reason. Who am I to question who I am, how I've been made, or how my life's been designed in the face of the Creator? I learned through the destructive behavior of my peer group to suppress my intelligence, my interest in different things from the norms, and that keeping quiet about myself and my personality was worth sacrificing to avoid public torment and harassment. I learned quickly after graduating high school that my social education was extremely awful and I have been focused on undoing the damage since then. In discussing these experiences with others, I've been basically shocked to realize that I suffered through these with an amazing amount of privilege on my side, being English speaking, heterosexual, CIS gendered, male, and white in a conservative and largely socially ignorant town. I can't imagine how much more difficult my experiences could have been otherwise. One of the hardest skills for me to learn (and keep developing) is learning to talk about myself beyond a superficial level with any degree of openness. Having spent the majority of my life being socially conditioned to stay silent, and knowing there are countless others in my situation, I believe that this silence needs to be broken.

We, as radicals and punks, need more efforts like this book. Creating a dialogue and breaking down the stigma against mental health issues is critical for us, especially since the communities around these interests are incredibly creative. Generally speaking, intelligent, analytical, and creative-minded people are more likely to suffer from depression (and similar illnesses) than others who are differently minded. Since hardcore/punk and radicalism are communities full of very creative people, that means a higher percentage of our community is prone to suffering similarly to myself (or much worse) than compared to normal society. Having little to no precedence for dealing with this within punk/hardcore and radicalism is a dire problem, especially considering there are many of us who deal with these issues every day and feel as though nobody cares, or would care, about it. I don't know what the methods are, or could be, and I'm not sure of how to enact them, but every effort we can make as community members to destigmatize mental/cognitive disorders, those who suffer from them, and viable treatments (i.e. skepticism towards holistic, pharmaceuticals, psychiatric therapy, etc.), the more likely we are to enable the positive health of others.

Although I have been privileged to have even a short term of treatment and extremely fortunate enough to have supportive friends, the determination to keep confronting my disorders, and years of experience doing so, I feel my efforts to remain healthy still remain a huge (and at times, insurmountable) challenge. I honestly take my life and my health one day at a time, with the expectations of doing so for the rest of my life. What I feel is the biggest clusterfuck of suffering from depression and anxiety, is that the symptoms of these diseases cause cognitive blind spots to life beyond them. My primary challenge is to develop better awareness of who I am and who I strive to be while in anxious or depressed states. If there's one positive thing about my life with mental illness, it's that I've earnestly grown to become the incredibly strong person I am, and the incredible potential behind that in becoming a better person, friend, and ally—good health permitting.

I became a panicking mess.

Calvin Chaos

First of all, I'm no authority on anything, I just read, talk to people, think a lot, and do the best I can. If you're in doubt about anything here, be my guest and do some research like I did. Google is your friend!

I've never tried to write with this kind of mania before. It reminds me of trying to be a substitute teacher for a high school class, while three people wave their arms in front of you like NBA players. Regardless, from what I've seen, a lot of mental patients don't shed much light on their experience, which brings a lot of misunderstandings and confusion from friends, family & co-workers, so I'm gonna share a little bit of my story, since I've been asked.

In 2004 I was diagnosed with bipolar disorder, and since then I've also been diagnosed with panic disorder. My main problems are mania, chronic anxiety, and panic attacks. Since you're probably not familiar with any of these first hand I'll give a little short explanation.

1. Bipolar disorder; formerly known as manic-depression. Professionals in the mental health field thought "manic depression" was too confusing of a label so they renamed it "bipolar"

disorder (MUCH CLEARER!?). A lot of famous people have had this, including such household names as Jimi Hendrix, Ozzy Osbourne, Marilyn Monroe, etc. Google "famous bipolar people" some time.

2. Panic Disorder is the more disruptive version of anxiety disorder, characterized by recurring panic attacks, and high anxiety in-between attacks. Patients will often experience these attacks suddenly, at unexpected times, and in familiar situations. The patient is often left dreading the next attack after a panic episode, which creates a "revolving door" of terror.

In my case, having the above problems also led to agoraphobia, but I won't touch on that too much because people are pretty familiar with it. Unfortunately this isn't going to be a big success story as I'm in the middle of wrestling with these problems, but I'll share what I think might be relevant to another patient, or their family.

My trouble with mental illness starts at the root, with the genes in my family. I have other bipolars in my family to reference when I fight my own problems. Unfortunately the mania is pretty crazy in our family, and so far not one patient I've seen has been able to handle it without the symptoms at least partially destroying their lives. The root of this, in my opinion, is confusion.

When a patient with bipolar, or panic is alone they can do plenty. In social situations however, perceptions get jumbled and when tact is needed, it's easy for a bipolar to fail in the light. From my observations, myself and most other patients who have more active mania than "depression" (the "depressive" phase isn't actual depression, that's the clinical term for the "low," as opposed to "high" stage of the bipolar cycle) are easily confused, easily irritated, hard to understand at random times, and paranoid.

These things might sound pretty normal, but imagine not being able to rely on the information about your environment that your brain is telling you. Right now I'm "lucid," and I can be understood. But in fifteen minutes, or an hour, or in the morning I will be trapped in a distorted version of this world like Alice in Wonderland. Would you want me as head of your house hold, or working for your company?

The brain is the tool that you use all other tools with. If you're trying to build with a broken hammer, the work will be sub-standard. In the same way, constantly working with such a clouded mind is an easy way to gradually slop up everything in your life.

I've probably always had panic disorder, but when I was a young child the symptoms mostly manifested as creativity, "magical" social skills (low effort), clowning, and excess energy. As you get older, bipolar changes. First it "gets triggered", meaning the symptoms become disruptive enough to be diagnosed (and often require treatment), then some time down the line (usually around retirement time) the symptoms drop in severity and change again.

With each of these changes comes a variation in how the mind works, confusion, and a lot of mental adaptation. Often family members are confused, and annoyed by the patient. Bipolar patients often seem as "normal" as anybody else for a few hours a day. Only through a patients' abnormally fluctuating, and elevated, or swinging moods can others see signs of a problem. Even then, the symptoms often camouflage well as "personality traits," further confusing the patient and everybody else.

If you have to deal with a bipolar person in your regular routine, try to remember they are probably just as bothered and annoyed by their symptoms as you are. That understanding goes a long way. If you can't remember that, when the person in off in their manic world, imagine they have an involuntary IV pumping hard liquor and drugs into them at random times through the day, every day. My symptoms are that strong, so I imagine a lot of other people's are too. The need for this understanding is just to help to deal with this person with a minimum of drama.

While I'm still in your world let me give a little bit of my story before I end.

When I was fifteen years old I had my first panic attacks. I woke up one day before work and my heart was beating so hard, that my family saw my pulse from across the room. I kept having them, because it didn't stop. About forty-eight hours later, I was still having heart palpitations, pouring sweat, shaking, and hyperventilating. I had been to work and to the store twice like this and nothing changed. I went to the county hospital.

The doctor and nurses at the hospital told me just to relax and stop driving myself so hard. They didn't tell me what a panic attack was. This is typical, most panic disorder patients I've met had similar experiences, and thus were not able to "nip the problem in the bud."

I didn't have another panic attack until I was twenty-one. This time the attacks weren't as strong, but they were very frequent. Every day I began to have hours of random terror for "no reason." I didn't know anything more than your average person about mental illness, and nothing about panic disorder (or bipolar). Friends and family had nothing to say about my concerns. I was on my own with no information. I decided just to use will-power to overcome the problem, and to force myself to live surrounded by crowds of people. In my case this never worked. (I've been in ten plus bands, worked at the world's biggest airport, worked labor, retail, had supervisory and managerial jobs, been in the punk rock scene for fifteen plus years, and I'm more anxious than I ever thought I would be.)

My disorientation and mania increased more slowly than the panic, which helped it to creep up and take me by surprise. It's always bad for bipolars when that happens, because you become so disoriented that people start to agree that you're "crazy." Since you're not ALWAYS "crazy" though, you look like a faker.

Back to the story though . . .

As the years went by, my moods began to destabilize, which is normal for bipolar patients. Everybody around me noticed and commented before I did. This was added onto my now daily recurring panic attacks, accompanied by some kind of anger episodes. People who had been down with me for years suddenly grouped together to try and make my life hard. The stronger the symptoms, the more I had social problems.

I tried to be brave like when I was younger and I got more scared for no reason. I tried to be more articulate, but in my mind I became less coherent more often. I tried to avoid all drama, but I was too disoriented to know when I was acting off compared to what people around me were doing. I had entered the "am I going crazy phase."

After a few years of living like this, working hard, partying hard, and refusing to give up, stay on the mat, or cave in to pressure from "friends" or peers, I started feeling burnt out and exhausted. I had no idea how to be happy in life any more.

In 2003 I tried to join the Army. I thought that only constant work would keep me stable. When I was at work, I was mad and anxious every day. This was a daily problem, year round. I was violent around this period and for years to come, but having an approachable demeanor assured that I had a growing stable of contacts and wanna-be "friends." This was even more confusing, because it gave me a little limited feeling of "normalcy" and false social security.

After taking the ASVAB, physical and scholastic tests for the military I was informed two steps away from shipping out, that I was "text book bipolar" (there is no such thing if you were wondering, but close enough) by the Army doctor. Since I lived in Chicago, they were able to refer me to the free county hospital, to enter a mental treatment facility. I got on a waiting list and nine months later I was going to a mental health clinic.

My experience at this clinic was a mixed bag. For the first few years I was happy, because I was over-medicated. I felt like a teenager again (just with slightly worse nerves). Much of my bravery was back, and my old personality had just been hibernating under there. Unfortunately a bitter, angry, violent, manic person running around over-medicated was never going to work out in the long run. Eventually I started hallucinating (a blue demon walked beside me every where and goaded me), and I had to come off of Klonopin, the only drug that had ever worked for my panic. My job and independence went bye bye, so did my bands. I was lucky that I had always been overly giving, and my partner was willing to look out for me while I was down. I distanced myself from most of my friends and associates, having seen before that they couldn't handle the confusion of bipolar or panic disorder much better than I, the patient could.

This social withdrawal is common among patients and it's a double-edged sword. When I've withdrawn socially in my life, it has been for "damage control." I like to avoid all drama unless I see a reason to be forceful against somebody else, or I risk drama to explain a point, then stroke the other persons ego. I almost never veered from my little "drama code." I've had a lot of associates point out how they never had an argument with me, yet I've been violent sometimes with other people when it wasn't warranted. They think the whole thing is my personality, however briefly. No one seems to remember that I'm a mental patient in a permanent sense.

My time at the mental hospital made me never want to go to another one. I'll skip most details for brevity. I promptly got constipated with three square meals a day (I was only used to one meal, typical poor punk), plus the new meds they gave me. My old reliable Klonopin had some bad withdrawal too. People with experience say it's worse than crack or heroin withdrawal. I'll take their word for it. I don't know why anybody would take it for fun.

In the months after I was released from the mental hospital, I had to taper myself off of the meds they gave me. My pancreas and liver were giving me trouble. I went to the hospital to get a second opinion a few weeks after I started throwing up blood, and they said my psych meds needed to be adjusted. My doctor at the clinic wouldn't do it, so after a few more weeks I started tapering myself off, which is potentially fatal. I wasn't going to let them kill me while I was trying to fix the problem. This is also normal fare for a lot of patients. Horror stories among mental patients abound for a reason, I came to find out. The field is a little primitive.

It was about two years before I could pee clearer than dark orange, and again I was alone with my problem; no leverage, no power . . . only an unending, invisible battle before me. I was just glad I didn't die from pancreatitis, and continued to try and "fix my brain." I was a little bit peeved, but what are you going to do?

After that experience I switched clinics and finally started getting decent counseling. At the first clinic I originally was asked what I wanted from treatment. I told them no meds, just information and advice. They convinced me later to take meds by telling me that Klonopin was not addictive, and had no withdrawal. Go look up klonopin on Google and you'll know they lied right away. Always check the internet before you start meds. Some meds give you serious diseases (like Seroquel gives you diabetes), are not FDA approved, but are still prescribed. Be at least somewhat knowledgeable.

By the time I switched to the new clinic my young bubbly days were over, and I was wary of everybody, extra bitter, disoriented, holding back rage so I decided to say as little as possible and be very careful. This was a good decision, especially for a bipolar person. We have a tendency to be overly dramatic, since our brains try to blow everything out of proportion (especially during mania). I went through CBT (Cognitive Behavioral Therapy) for the anxiety, and was given much help in changing my perspectives, which was invaluable and continues to help me make what slow progress I can right now.

I have made some changes and learned some things, but I have a long way to go. I finally got my temper back close to normal (even though it still gets out of hand and I'm way too touchy), but the mania still confuses the hell out of me, and the panic attacks come daily. My relationships with family have always been strained, and there's a lot of distance and confusion. I don't know if I have any friends. The ones who call themselves my friends have all stabbed me in the back in my eyes since I turned twenty-one, and I'm thirty-four now. Since I have high mania, I know that's probably garbage, but I can't tell for sure. Doctors and therapists finally told me two years ago that I would always be bipolar and there was no cure. I had heard that from a few sources before, but when they tell you to your face and it already messed up your whole life, it's a different story.

Having seen other, older, patients who had been married, doctors, lawyers, with children etc., who ended up in similar situations to mine, I'm by no means happy about having to travel down this road for life. I mean at first you think you're just an idiot, so then you have the hope that you'll wise up and get on top of the problem. Well since I won't commit suicide I just have to keep working on it. Hopefully something I wrote will strike a chord in your mind and help you with some clarity on your own problem. I'm drifting back into Wonderland, so I'm gonna go now before I give "normal" people more gossip fuel.

Music, Medication, and My Experiences in the Spirit World

"Catherine Earnshaw"

I'm an artist living in Bushwick, New York. Last spring, on my day off, I headed over to Heaven Street, the record store in my neighborhood. I saw a flyer for "Punk Rock, Mental Illness and Recovery—A Talk Given by 'Crusty' Craig Lewis." I didn't know who this "Crusty" might be but I thought "This sounds awesome."

I have always been fascinated by the connections between music and mental illness and how music, or being part of a music scene in particular, can heal what ails the mind. A music scene, or any artistic community for that matter, can be a place where certain issues are tolerated and accepted that wouldn't be in normal life.

I went to the talk and I was taken aback at what Craig had to say. It was incredible to hear someone talking openly about his life and from a place of honesty in which shame wasn't an issue. It can take a lot of courage to share something so personal but the fact is that this is something that helps people.

Craig said he was putting together his zine *You're Crazy*, and I said "Hey, that's me!" My entire life, people have said "You're crazy."

In a certain sense I am an extremely reserved person and on the other hand I am hyper and can scream or burst into tears very easily.

I'm not afraid of being emotional in public. I think it should happen more often. I don't like hiding things. There have been so many times in New York City when I was walking down the street with tears streaming down my face whether from some kind of sadness or just because the music I was listening to was so beautiful. Sometimes people stare or ask "Why are you crying?" and sometimes they don't. But I don't notice because I'm just in my own world. It's who I am. At school I was always "Cathy the crazy girl" or "Crazy Cathy." When I was little my friend's father always called me "The Screamer" because I used to have screaming contests with the other kids (maybe that's why I like punk and noise so much now).

By the time I was twenty I had heard "You're crazy" so many times, I went to a psychiatrist. It was terrifying for me because I was so convinced there was something wrong with me. I was convinced I was fucked up. But after speaking with him for a half-hour, he just looked at me and said, "There is nothing wrong with you. You're a very stable person." I was shocked!

So my whole life of being regarded as a crazy person was . . . crap? I often think, since I'm from a small town in Massachusetts a couple of hours from Salem, that in a past life I must have been a witch. A witch is a girl you're not sure of; you don't know what's in her head. Why does she act the way she does? Is she in contact with spirits? In school plays I always got cast as witches. I'm glad it's not olde times anymore- I probably would have been burned at the stake. I'm thinking of Hole's song from *Live Through This*, "Softer, Softest . . ." She sings "Burn the witch, burn the witch . . . just bring me back her head . . ."

However, I never want to give up my head, or my mind the way it is. I have had high anxiety for most of my life. A few years ago I tried medication, something I had always resisted. I agreed to try it and now I'm taking an anti-anxiety medication every day. I have to say that I have mixed feelings about medication.

I think music can really help with anxiety and any other issues as everyone in this zine already knows. My father is a classical musician and he always tells a story about Beethoven. There was a woman Beethoven knew. She was a wealthy woman whose son had just died.

For a long time she wasn't able to cry. She wasn't able to speak at all. She was just trapped, paralyzed, and silenced. Beethoven was called to go to her house and play piano. As soon as he started playing she started crying for the first time since her son died. She just sat there and listened and after a while she was able to speak again.

I know music can save someone's life. There have been so many times when I feel like music saved me. It's a way of speaking to each other that doesn't involve any crap. When there is no crap and no shame, you can heal and you can heal others. It helps you feel less alone. I definitely think my anxiety can be isolating and it's something I have to fight against. I am thinking of a line from Interpol's post-punk masterpiece *Turn on the Bright Lights*. He sings, "You come here to me, we'll collect those lonely parts and set them down." On a B-side from that same album, he says again, "When you lost your nurses, I found you a doctor in me." Listening to the right song is like getting a blood transfusion.

I'm reading a book right now called *The Temple of Shamanic Witchcraft: Shadows, Spirits and the Healing Journey*. Historically shamans have been society's healers. There's a paragraph which states:

> Many shamans feel they are chosen or called by the spirits directly, and learn their arts from the spirits. A traumatic experience can induce the contact. Some might simply start seeing and conversing with spirits. It is sometimes connected with madness, as certain individuals go wild and mad, living apart from the tribe. If they learn to listen to the spirits, they gain the survival skills they need and the magical skills to heal and help others, returning as a shaman. Those in traditional Western society are most apt to think the spirit worker is completely crazy.

I'm fine now with people saying "You're crazy." In fact, if no one said it to me anymore, I would be concerned about myself. I am this way for a reason and today it's an empowerment to me to say, "Yeah, you know what? I AM fucking crazy. I AM fucked up." And I wouldn't want it any other fucking way.

The Music of my Madness

Christina

I am going to be honest. This is not my best writing, but it is some of my most sincere. I didn't feel like editing it because I hate thinking about this shit so please forgive the run-on sentences and grammar errors. I just thought it was important for me to contribute.

Editor's note: I volunteered to edit stories in this compilation, so I am now editing my own story a year later. I cleaned up some of the grammar, but tried to maintain the syntax and sincerity of the original writing.

I have struggled with bipolar disorder since my memory begins, but I had my first psychotic episode when I was twenty-one. My child-hood was perfect in many ways: we had money, my parents remain happily married to this day, my younger sister and brother are very sweet, and my parents are very loving and supportive. Unfortunately, I am a wreck and I was always a wreck. From baby-hood on, I had extreme, truly indescribable tantrums that were physically and verbally abusive to anyone near me. I would just become possessed; my senses would overwhelm me, my head would flood and I would literally want to die to end the pain I was in . . . this is before I even entered elementary school. My parents did not know what to do with me and so, for my siblings' safety and my mom's, my mom (who stayed home with us) would put me in my room until my dad got home whenever I would fly into one of my tantrums. For some reason I was less defiant with my father and he would pet my head and read to me until I fell asleep on those bad days. Although I remember my childhood with somewhat of a gray haze, I remember my dad's compassion clearly. To this day, having someone I love pet my head is still one of the most calming coping mechanisms that I rely on.

Once I entered school, I struggled severely. I didn't learn to read until I was in the second grade. My younger sister (who is two years younger) actually helped teach me to read. I struggled academically through elementary school and middle school, but was often noticed for my imagination, compassion, and loud mouth. In sophomore year of high school, after years of being labeled lazy and a bad kid, I was diagnosed with ADHD and general reading learning disabilities. At the time of that diagnosis, the psychiatrist warned my mother that I was really emotionally and psychologically unstable and needed therapy. He saw the beginnings of my bipolar disorder, but, without any major episodes, he couldn't diagnose it.

I spent sophomore year in and out of doctor's offices, on and off depression pills. Because I was bipolar, the anti-depressants caused bizarre reactions a few days after I started taking them. I would swing into full blown psychosis, but each medication would cause different manifestations of psychosis. An example of this: On Wellbutrin, I suddenly had a psychotic break in the shower one night, a few days after starting the medication. I was convinced I could see a dead person and she was trying to kill me. I ran through my house naked, screaming for help. That night, my mom clothed me in her pajamas, kicked my dad out of bed, and I slept with her in my parent's bed. One can imagine how difficult this was for a teenager to be experiencing as well as for her family to be watching. It was really fucking scary and unnerving. It was also incredibly embarrassing. I had the luck or misfortune—I still don't know which one it is—of having a mother who grew up around the mentally ill and retarded. Her parents were psychiatrists and, at one point, worked for the state of

Ohio treating the criminally insane. This helped her not overreact to me running through the house naked, screaming about dead people and it helped her be compassionate about not hospitalizing me. My mom knew what the hospital really meant for patients. At the same time, my treatment was perhaps postponed because private practice psychiatrists think about their patients for fifteen minutes while the patient sits in front of them and then they move on with their day. I really appreciate not ever being hospitalized throughout my treatment; very few people as sick as me have had such a luxury.

By college, my depression was becoming more and more severe and, proportionately, my drinking became heavier and heavier. Then it happened. My last semester of college, I experienced full blown mania. I was wild and excited. Everything was incredible and I could accomplish anything. No actions had consequences and I felt absolutely free. But, true to my illness, I fell into a deep depression following this manic episode. I remained on this rollercoaster of illness for years—I would go up and then down and then up again and so on.

When I was twenty-two, I got married to a man I had been with from the time I was sixteen years old. We loved each other, but were truly unprepared for what was going on with me and what was to come. A few months after our wedding, I sank into a deep, catatonic depression that no spouse expects at all and especially not as a newlywed. It was incredibly tough on him and it put deep strains on our relationship, but he stood by me. I quit my job. It was the first time I had been unemployed since I was fifteen years old. He came home one day and found my suicide note when he was changing the sheets on the bed. Another day he came home and I was wasted on vodka and wine. I ate intermittently. I slept in bizarre patterns. I barely spoke and rarely left bed. The only comfort I could find was in writing, drawing, and reading Norse mythology. Enough was enough and I was back in doctor's offices. This time I had a diagnosis, though. This time I was bipolar II. Similar to bipolar I, bipolar II could kind of be simplified by saying that you experience the highs and lows but generally maintain being a functional person (not to say it isn't a very difficult disease to live with—it is just characteristically less extreme). I was put on 200 milligrams of Lamictal through a slow process (one can't just take high dosages of Lamictal immediately because of a strong risk for a fatal allergic reaction called Steven Johnson's disease). A couple months after this first diagnosis, I went into a full blown psychotic state and was diagnosed as bipolar I. I was paranoid; I was OCD (For example, I had to say certain phrases to people or I thought they would die); I didn't eat; I exercised too much, etc. My doctor offered me a few options for anti-psychotics to put a lid on the mania. By this point, my mania had progressed to a severe level and I was so obsessed with my weight I told her I wouldn't take anything associated with weight gain. She prescribed Geodon. I now know that Geodon is often used as a last resort medication because its side effects can be so severe. I, unfortunately, am very medication sensitive and experienced every side effect on the giant paragraph list of side effects that accompanies prescribed medication except the side effect of sudden, unexpected death. When I complained, my doctor told me I was just being med non-compliant. I dropped ten pounds. in a week from muscle rigidity spiking my metabolism and loss of appetite. Five hours after taking the med, I would lose consciousness for three to four hours. I stayed on it a few months and then gave up on it and her. I was off to find another doctor.

Looking for a mental health provider in a private practice is awful if you have a severe mental illness. In New Hampshire (I don't know if this is generalizable to other states), they can deny you if they feel you are too risky. So, I learned to lie. I just didn't disclose my past disordered eating, my body dismorphia, suicidal ideation, substance abuse, the cutting habit I had in middle school, and so forth. I disclosed my diagnosis, my past sexual abuse which had caused PTSD and panic disorder, and the meds I was prescribed. I finally landed a good psychiatrist and an awesome therapist who I have seen off and on for the past five years.

Today, I am unmedicated—much to the dismay of my mental health providers. I am going through a divorce that was caused partly by my mental illness and partly because of other factors. I see my therapist regularly. I drink. I smoke. I do drugs. I do what I deem necessary to survive and I am making it work. Despite being unmedicated for almost a full year now, I have not had any major episodes. A lot of this is because my home life is more stable than it has been in the past and a lot of it is just luck. Med non-compliance is very common among people with bipolar disorder, especially BP I. We tend to justify and negotiate with ourselves, especially during manic episodes.

I am no longer active in punk. I still have a lot of friends that I love very much who are and I still love punk music, but we all know punk is much more than a music genre. I have generally left the scene. I think it saved my life in high school and in my twenties because it gave me a world that, for the first time, I didn't feel weird or bizarre in. I felt normal, pretty, and talented. I lost myself in the noise and stimulation of punk. I played in a band that meant everything to me and it was a great outlet for a lot of my pain. Some of my lyrics dealt directly with my mental illness and pain. As I struggle to regain my life after the past five years of illness and turmoil, though, I have to distance myself. It is too easy for me to sink into self-destruction when I get too close to punk. It's too alluring to completely disregard my well-being and just drink myself into nothing. So now, I live in a house with some of my closest friends and my boyfriend; I am completing my master's degree in library science; and I am doing my best to survive. People always say, "At least you have your health." Sometimes they say it to me and I chuckle because they have no idea how out of control my health is. Regardless, they are right. Nothing is better than the days I have where I feel "normal" or the weeks that I float in remission, when I don't feel out of control or at the mercy of my illness. I have been called a monster and unloveable because of my sickness. Today, I try to live for myself and I have a strong support group that reminds me of what I have to offer this world. A recent study I read in *Bipolar Disorders,* an academic journal dedicated to research about bipolar disorder, said that people with BP I typically die three decades before the average person because of a myriad of health complications and suicide. I hope I beat the odds.

The little advice I can give at this point in my life, because I have done anything but conquered my illness, is to educate oneself. Find the prestigious academic publications that deal with your sickness and learn the language and the research and the drugs. I am lucky because, as a librarian, I have access to a lot of publications that are not immediately available to everyone. I read *Bipolar Disorders*, a peer-reviewed scientific publication; I have read a recent textbook published on neurobiology specifically related to bipolar disorder. I read recent lawsuits dealing with the drugs I take. Wikipedia is an awesome resource to begin with if you are confused (look at the bibliography for resources). NAMI is an awesome resource. If you are in college, you probably have access to a lot of academic publications in databases or as print or eJournals. You can also request specific articles or books through Interlibrary Loan if you don't have access at your library. If you aren't a student in a college, check the closest public college or community college. Often the libraries of public colleges will grant public access to their databases and e-Journals on-campus with a guest pass. Some private universities also offer access to their electronic collections on-campus to guests, but I suggest calling ahead if the policy is not explicitly stated on their website. The reason I say educate yourself, though, is that you are your own best advocate. Speak up for yourself and assert your needs and goals with your mental health providers.

Finally, find memoirs and zines of people dealing with mental illness. I wasn't going to contribute to this publication because I am sick of thinking about being sick so I avoid it at all costs. Then, I thought about how much comfort I found reading *Madness: A Bipolar Life* by Marya Hornbacher and I decided to contribute last minute. I guess, in some ways, my attraction to memoirs about people who are sick like me is the whole misery loves company thing, but I also just think that it's important to contextualize oneself. A coping mechanism I have developed to deal with my constant suicidal ideation is to refuse anonymity. I can't remember what sociologist observed this, but he identified anonymity as being a significant perception in those who attempted or committed suicide. So, when all I can think about is putting a gun in my mouth or slitting my throat or slicing open my femoral artery, I read other people's stories. When I feel like this, I also think about the people who love me. I have always rationalized that I am more of a burden dead than I am alive. If I am alive, people have the choice to deal or not to deal with me. If I am dead, I am just a ghost that haunts them for the rest of their lives.

I really don't know how to end this story because there really isn't an end to it. Update over a year later: I have now been clean for over a year. A little after writing this story, I went into a complete tailspin (which I kind of smile about now because I can see the symptoms in my writing). When I say tailspin, I mean it. I was in a mixed episode. (A mixed episode is when a BP person experiences simultaneous manic and depressive symptoms; it is considered the most dangerous state because of the vulnerability to suicide and high risk behavior.) I was up and down. I tried to drive to Ohio to off myself (I have no idea why I choose Ohio). I devastated myself financially. I took an incomplete from school. I binged on drugs and alcohol. I stopped working. I could go on, but, for the sake of time, let's just say that I was a complete mess. I had to make a decision again. I had to choose to completely stay away from substances I abused. I had to choose to get healthy and I had to choose to be disciplined about my health.

As I said before, I have now been clean for a year. I make daily efforts to pay attention to my moods so I remain self-aware instead of in a perpetual state of flight. I have almost repaired myself financially, although it will take years to truly repair what I did in a couple months. My major concern at the moment is changing therapists. The woman I have been seeing for years doesn't have hours that work with my new work schedule. The idea of having to switch therapists is so devastating that I have been procrastinating—that's my go-to flight response kicking in.

I will end by reiterating what I said over year ago about educating and advocating for yourself: it is truly paramount and the investment of time to educate yourself will continue to pay off.

Mad Love and Rage

Eric Blitz

R ight from the start of life, I had to come to terms with being different, a misfit. First I was born to a couple who, though being Alsatian originally, were in a small city in the Midwest United States with all the trappings of the South. They had North African blood and there was poverty and drugs, and what I would learn later was that they were full of culture that would come to play a more significant role in my life. That said, I was put up for adoption, to a couple who, to this day, are more than devout Christians, support the right wing and, being quite well off, reek of class and race opinions that would, and still do, make me feel ill just at the thought.

Shortly after I was adopted, it was found out that I had been born breech and my umbilical cord had strangled me, cutting the air off just long enough to leave me with a disabled left side of my body. One of my earliest memories was of my adoptive parents telling me that they kept me rather than "returning" me because Dad had the finances and Mom had been a nurse and would be able to provide for my "special" needs. This being the 1960s, I can only imagine that medical mishaps likely went unreported and my "parents" finding society to be going in a way they did not approve of, I was in their eyes in a "great position."

There were also varying, conflicting stories that my birth parents were either too poor or had too many kids or that my birth father had died. Years later, I was able to unearth birth records through my own investigation and learned that my parents had been youngish—my mother likely in her teens—from the Alsace-Lorraine, and that I had been born addicted to opiates.

Whether at home or at school, I got the idea that life was not only my family but other kids I met delivering a series of put downs and put ons. It was not long before the fighting with other kids, teachers, and my family would start. You see, at a very young age, I found music. I would sit in front of the stereo entranced at what was coming out at me. Music moved me, made me feel there was a world beyond where I was. I wanted to know everything about music—the people, the instruments, the culture. I wanted to feel. The kids at school would taunt me because on Monday morning as everyone talked about sports or the weekend game, no one wanted to hear about the music I had listened to or caught a glimpse of on TV. Suddenly, I became weirder.

My only solace was a grandmother who, though a generation older than my adoptive parents, seemed to have cultivated a zeal for life that had skipped them. She enjoyed playing bridge, drinking whiskey and water, and smoking Camels. She had many fond memories of seeing the "big bands" in her youth and would speak of Gene Krupa, Louie Bellson, and Chick Webb, drummers all. This is a good time to say that as far back as I could remember, I was drawn to the DRUMS. I realized guitars and other instruments were not possible to handle with my left arm, but I knew that drums moved the band. I had been given toy drums and would blow through the paper heads and spend days making "new" drumheads. I found the music of Elvis and my parents' *American Graffiti 50's* soundtrack soon giving way to the Stones, Velvet Underground, The Stooges, The New York Dolls, and later still to more avant-garde sounds, the post-punk, industrial, noise, and sound experiment genres. And the constant of old blues on the AM radio I had.

I was given a real drum set at seven years old and was told I had to take lessons. I began doing nothing else. Soon at the corner market, I was hipped to *Creem* magazine and Lester Bangs. I found out more about other groups, especially coming out of NYC and their love of the Beats and the French avant-garde. I found out about visual art, performance, and literature. I especially liked the Dada movement. All this made an even bigger gulf with my family and the kids at school and around the neighborhood. Now I was a cripple, a freak, and I had nothing in common with anyone around me. Soon the fighting at home and everywhere reached a breaking point and my parents sent me to a string of psychologists. When therapy did not turn me into what my parents wanted, I was put in a thirty-day psych ward. Mostly for my parents just wanting, needing a break.

I found just a few friends, most of whom were older. I found I was not alone—before I knew it a whole world opened to me, when I first found punk, or it found me. I met a few people and made some friends. Of course, my parents disapproved. Now, a lucky thing would happen; I met a local artist who was in a punk/no wave group called Circle X who took me under his wing. I learned about life through a different lens, my friend Bruce in talking to me not as a child, made me open myself up to questioning everything. I came to find another spiritual path, Thelema, that spoke to me more than the tradition I was brought up in. I found that after all the years of abuse from people at large that there was a class divide in the U.S. In a word, I had become politicized.

It was normal for people to yell at me, push me over, beat me up. One day a car pulled up and I was dragged inside by the passengers— two men and a woman. I was driven away to an unfamiliar area and violated. I was still a boy who had not even had sex at this time—this act had a lifelong effect on me. Bruce had by this time moved away to Paris, then New York City. On becoming a teenager I too bought a one way bus ticket to New York City. At last I was in the hub of all I ever dreamed of. Being a young teen who had never been taught anything on how to take care of myself, here I was in a city, and though I had a few friends, I was on my own. My social security had yet to start, and even after it did there was still a part of me that was vulnerable yet full of rage. I spent time on the streets and soon I found smack and hustling. By the time my S.S. kicked in, my life was already consumed by drugs and sex for money. No matter how many songs or stories speak of this, it never becomes truly "normal;" it takes its toll.

I did, in all this, get to take part in the early days of the New York punk scene, though I found through my prior drum teachers I still had a love of jazz. Political and consumed with thoughts of love and rage, I found when punk gave way to no wave and the jazz loft scene dovetailed, I was in heaven. I played in bands, saw shows, art openings, readings, and yet the drugs grew more out of control. I was forced to grow up fast and I must thank a few lovely trans/pansexuals who looked after me.

In the course of my time on the streets, I found myself again raped. I was at this time told everything was part of "it"—the scene, the art— lies to keep the victims questioning themselves. There were things that made me feel crazy, and there were people ready to pounce on that and make me feel crazy for completely different reasons, that usually came with an agenda. I did a lot of stuff in the name of "art" that was totally demeaning. Often in circles I traveled I would meet and be around and make music and art with some great people. However, as things became hip to the bougies, there were people around who were ready to use and take advantage of you. By the end I had gone out to LA to make a record with one of the musicians I really liked, and I spent seven years in LA. Same drill.

It was not long before I ended up in rehab. It was then facing all the years of destruction that I found out I have Hepatitis C. I had already seen HIV take out most of my friends. Even Bruce had passed on in the mid-90s. I re-met an artist friend, Valerie in California, who I'd known in NYC and who was now HIV positive, and we were married. We knew one of us would not get out alive. She eventually crossed over, but not before preparing me to face some of my demons.

Life however still had the troubles of losing or not being able to find a home or people who are ready to use and abuse you. Valerie and I returned to NYC in 2000, realizing that the art and music we were both passionate about was still there and, even with gentrification, is still in the eyes of a few.

I had wanted to devote my music work into saying something political, and I wanted to, at long last, explore jazz in all its forms, and I have. Before Valerie's passing, I was told that she had brought me this far, yet my true love and soul mate awaited. She was selfless in that way.

The issues of abandonment I suffered from now were at a peak. Grieving never fully ends, but at the end of the initial shock, the woman I had always known was my equal came into my life. I had known of her through an underground film clip, performances, and a few mutual acquaintances. I thought I would be alone forever, having no skills at courting a woman after ten years of marriage, but I fell in love with Jenny, and she with me, and she is now my wife. A kindred damaged-and-tossed-about soul, she understands me and takes me as I am, and I her. We live in an abandoned coffin factory converted to an art space with our rats and cats, and a few like-minded housemates. We have both had our demons arise and we have learned to accept them and to grow each day. Recently, I was told by my counselor I had PTSD. When I told Jenny, she laughed and said "I thought you already knew." I had thought PTSD was something that only affected soldiers, but it also affects those of us who have been through these undeclared wars. All the things that had happened to me can send me off in my mind and cause a reaction in me.

I have found the saying "Know thyself" are words to live by. I make music now with a great group of people in Urchestra and Doll Hospital (both with Jenny), and my longest-ever standing gig is creating soundtracks with social/political artists such as Seth Tobocman or Eric Drooker. So I found a way to express myself—just go off and help the revolution. Music becomes not just entertainment but ritual, confrontation. In Doll Hospital, as well, Jenny and I explore our inner demons and passions together. It is true love and rage—mad love and rage.

Knives and Noise

Jenny "DevilDoll" Gonzalez-Blitz

Off-White Noise

There were times I could hear music no one else could. I'm not being flowery or metaphorical. For me, there were very literally sounds, or sometimes voices that crackled sharply out of empty air, rumbled through the ground or walls, or willed themselves into something out of static. My parents hated my childhood habit of putting the TV on the UHF station and . . . waiting.

There were early morning hours—like three or four AM where the sleeping, dark, and dead aluminum tract house erupted into a cacophony of murmurs and melody being tapped out on bits of metal, pots, soup cans, and pipes. There was also at one point the winter day, sun hanging low over the desert, where my ear lay against the dust and rock. IT had cracked my head with, choked to near unconsciousness because I wouldn't stop trying to scream or fight. Somewhere below, deep primal drum rhythms came up from the earth, from rivers of magma circling her core. In a haze, I turned my attention to those drums, to block out IT on top of me, ripping open what was for IT just another child orifice, I suppose. At least, that's what came to light when this incident was added to a manhunt already in progress.

The metal, the gongs, the drums, unbeknownst to me all trying to cosmically clue me in to where salvation would ultimately be found. But I had no idea of that trying to lose myself in the drum so I wouldn't feel the tearing. The teeth. The murder I assumed would follow (but obviously for whatever reason didn't.)

IT
    IT

stain stain stain stain stain stain stain stain stain stain stain
       IT
         IT
           IT

Bleed Bliss

Bleeding is at once alarming and comforting, a bright red scream shrieking the truth when every circumstance around you is trying to mold your very existence into lies. I'd actually learned that well before my desert encounter with IT, discovered that form of catharsis with a piece of broken glass in an elementary school playground. My mother saw this once and threatened to beat me with a belt if she ever caught me inflicting harm on myself. Inexplicably, as much as I was compelled to see damage, I was enormously resentful of anybody else being the cause of it. Uninvited, anyway. Keep things on the sly, under clothes.

R
E
THE TRUTH SHALL SCREAM YOU FREE
JARRED OF FALSE REALITY
A
S
E

Subculture as Spectacle

As much as I heard music no one else did, there were also songs and visions I insisted I inflict on the rest of the populace. Despite being one of those kids teachers and specialists label as "highly creative," I could not imagine a way to stop being morose, socially inept, or to give a fuck about it. I was drawn to the artistic and bizarre, "bohemia," "subculture," "underground." If something initially frightened me, my immediate follow-up reaction was to become obsessed with that thing, consumed by the thought of it. If my stepfather or mother (usually the latter) reacted negatively to my interest in something, I only became more intrigued because it was now taboo. Unfortunately in Arizona, it was next to impossible to find these things, and my most crucial link to any of this was a now-deceased Uncle. He would regale me with tales of New York streets and sub-culture as adamantly as my mother pressed us to forget our Hell's Kitchen roots, become laid back sun-loving Arizonans. (Due to my birth father's genes and surname, the other Arizonans did everything to sabotage that plan.)

No Maupin was my Uncle though, and his "Tales of the City" came with a price of blurred boundaries, inappropriate life-lessons (think how to turn a trick in a hotel lobby), and playing family members off of one another for what seemed to be his own personal amusement.

But the demons that clung to me from the desert and clawed my shoulders and arms (through my own hands) only amplified, while the ideas Uncle implanted either shouted back or chimed in with the ruckus. Eventually I returned to New York City, a hungry, artsy barely-adult with a cartoon devil whispering in one ear and another more insidious devil whispering in the other, with a more filial tone.

```
                        D                       bo
                        E                       u
                        V                       nd
            DEVIL < !   I       ! > DEVIL       aries ?
                        L                       ????????????
                        D
                        O
                        L
                        L
```

I crashed and burned through the art school I was naïve enough to believe would provide my family with a sense of legitimacy to my life goals and desires. Through personal exploration/experimentation with my native city, art gigs, art modeling, hospitalization, stripping and other equally demeaning ways society has devised of getting cheap, expendable labor from its throwaways. I learned how to fight on the physical while having zero understanding of how to defend myself in more intangible ways many predators find far more effective. My love for sharp objects grew. My Dad gave me a black military field knife, legal length to carry, and I practiced until I could draw and use it in a blink. I didn't want to brandish Blackie (yeah, I named it) at anyone. It would have been laughable in appearance, but not in usage. Blackie never took the stage with me the way those other, showier looking knives did.

On stage, with my band, I could be snotty, sulky, fiery, sexual, violent. I could ricochet off the drum kit and the amps, try to do the crabwalk from The Exorcist, and twirl my knives. Break from sarcastic lyrics into growls, hisses, glossolalia, intonations I didn't need to understand. Dingy beer-soaked punk bars and clandestine underground spots were Temples to Dionysus, the way all rock and roll is supposed to be, and I was a Maenad allowing actions and sounds to take me where they would. They in turn let me direct them to the jumping off point. I didn't care that I was as likely to rend myself apart as easily as the Pentheuses that awaited me at every turn.

Pentheus in Gracie Mansion.

Pentheus in the boardroom, seeking me after-hours in the backroom.

Pentheus in a blue uniform. Pentheus in a doctor's coat.

Pentheus trying to impress me with his trust fund, his imagined connections, his phony credibility.

Pentheus as a stalker telling me this was how everything happened in "the scene."

Pentheus as a boyfriend seeking danger and adventure in a "freaky" girlfriend. She would turn into a proper suburbanite on command.

Pentheus as a band mate wanting madness to the hilt onstage, where it would draw a crowd, but seeking to suppress and sabotage offstage, a mix of gloating privilege masked with crocodile concern.

Martial arts, knife techniques, they've gotten me out of a situation here and there, but I had no understanding of the verbal and emotional wars people wage every day, never did, really. I thought alternative (you can use that word as a commodity or its actual sense, it doesn't matter here) cultures, with their extolling of non-conformity and individual thought, would be the oasis, and in many ways they could be, to a point. But we were all born into the predominant culture, even if we made our way to the fringes. Even the punk scene in that point in time was probably as many people looking to put on a costume as it was people looking to reject the system that has continuously shit on us all.

Two members of my first band and an ex staged an "intervention" of sorts, walked me to Woodhull Hospital where I could be caged in with heavy numbing anti-psychotic medications, Risperdal, Seroquel and so on. Someone declared me "indigent" lest my inability to pay for the pleasure to keep it from happening.

Three days later, The Buildings were destroyed. One had nothing to do with the other, but for a brief period everyone around me also found their world as an uncertain, unsafe, decimated place. They didn't get placated with anti-psychotics. Instead, there was an equally unreal array of firefighters with flags, teary-eyed eagles, and even further decimation of countless people overseas, supposedly, on our behalf.

Was this really a story about punk? About searching for a freedom in bohemia, only to find that despite its solace, bohemia is also in an oppressor's chokehold? I didn't even touch on the takes figures identifying themselves as anyone from Jesus to Satan to Odin or Lilith gave me on everything. Or, how one day I no longer saw a point in knife-fucking simulations, or any other form of simulation, and went back into following those primal drums beating in the earth's core. Drums and lava, volcanically saving my life for a second time.

I'm happy now, but this isn't the happy ending. Because I'm not done yet.

Disease

Jessica Rosengrant

"**H**EY," she says to the back of my head, "I know you." She spits out the "know you" in a way that makes it sound like a secret code, an invitation. "You hang out with . . ." she trails off, squinting across the street, distracted by some small detail. She is right, of course. I nod, sucking on my teeth, mumbling an unintelligible response. "Well. Come on," she says, holding her hand out to me, eyebrows raised. I am startled. "Oh no," I tell her, sifting through my collection of excuses, "I was just waiting for the bus." But caught off guard, my words sound flimsy. Tucking my hair behind my ear and readjusting my hood, I look up at her and attempt a smile, but succeed only in an unintentional, half-assed smirk. I am an idiot—something she will remind me of at least once a day until we finally agree to part ways. I am a sucker. "Oh come on," she whines. "We're all going. See?" she insists, directing my attention to a group of people I vaguely recognize but hardly know. They are patiently waiting for her. I am cornered. Checkmate. I have nothing better to do and am rapidly losing interest in those "better" things as it is.

Walking arm in arm, our once guarded small talk has grown into full-fledged conversation. "And when I was twelve, do you know that my sister . . .?" I explain. "But really, I want to be a social worker," I declare. I am divulging personal information at a rate that most would find alarming, but she seems used to it. People tell her things, people look at her and think "this one will listen to me" and she soaks it up. Sitting here now, so far away from her, I can't find the exact moment when things went wrong. Weren't we going to be forever? Best friends? Things that seem important inevitably fizzle and fade. Forever isn't real.

Seven months after that first awkward encounter, we can't seem to get rid of each other. We don't try to. We are sitting in the dust by the train tracks, both eyeballing the ground, both trying to ignore the offensive heat of the sun sizzling on our skin like a freshly lit match. We have been making mental notes of our dreams and our goals; comparing them, expanding them. Now, we are silent. The weight of all the things we are wanting, the things we are needing, is so suffocating, so overpowering. We are surrounded by a vast expanse of nothing but the sound of our shallow but content breathing. I trace lines in the ground with my index finger. The lines are small, childish scribbles to help me ignore the scream of silence. I watch her as she inspects the splinters of a railroad tie. Her hair hangs down, obscuring the look of concentration, the scrunched up nose, the thin lips that I have come to know so well. She is always so fascinated by boredom.

"Well?" she asks, stretching her legs and arching her back as she stands. "Should we get out of here then?" I look up at her, shielding my face against the sun. She looks unreal in that light, like a shadow. "And go where?" I want to know. She pauses, giving this question a careful amount of consideration. Taking a moment to pick at a scab on her knee, she responds, "Anywhere we want, I guess." The gravity of this response is more than I was expecting. I look past her, down the tracks, trying to guess the distance between us and anything else. "Yeah?" I ask, looking back at her just in time to catch her look of exasperation as she sniffs out my hesitation. "Yeah."

We have been walking for hours. Days. Months even. An eternity. Each time she slows down, shows any inclination of stopping, I wait for her to catch her breath. I sit with her in the grass, resting my head on her shoulder. "We are almost there," she finally says. I shut my eyes, holding back my irritation, biting down on my tongue. She says that every day. I have been growing tired of her. We have spent so much time together now that we are repeating ourselves. Yes, I know that she is supposed to be someone. Yes, she knows the kind of pressure I am under. Our bickering has become a constant: we are competing with one another for the award that comes with getting the last word. Her cruelty shows more and more with each day, blotting out the person she was. My interest in what she has to say has diminished to something almost invisible.

I stand, pulling her up with me, letting her lean on me. "We're not even close," I tell her. Brushing the dirt from my hands, I repeat, "we're not even close." Stepping back onto the road, I lead the way and she follows like a scolded child. We stopped following the tracks miles ago, trading them in to parade blindly through an abandoned concrete wasteland. Turning around to judge our progress, I see her trip, stumble and gracelessly spill herself onto the asphalt. I stop, waiting again; agitated by the fact that she is forever slowing me down. "Are you coming or what?" I shout at her, my patience now completely drained. "I'm hurt," she tells me, "I need your help." I am astonished. She has never admitted to any weakness that I can recall. I walk back to her, slowly, carelessly, and bend down to observe the damage. I would not have thought that she would break so easily, but broken she is. Her ankle is swollen, hinting already at the awful color that will fill it in and her skinned palms are turned towards me. "I need your help," she repeats.

She looks up at me, her expression matter of fact, but only barely masking her fear. "You'll have to carry me," she says.

I could turn now, walk away, leave her crumpled on the ground, but I don't. It is so hard to abandon her. We have traveled so far, seen so much, side by side.

I drop my bag and crouch down, arms wrapped around my knees so that we are eye to eye. "Please?" she asks and I quietly concede. I cannot leave her, not here. We bring only the things that we will need and that I am able to carry—a pack of playing cards that is missing the queen of hearts, two lighters (one already spent), an empty notepad, and a dry pen. The pile of things that we will have to leave behind so that I can support her weight, the things we have deemed unnecessary after much discussion, growing by the second and scattering in the wind. "How long do I have to carry you?" I want to know. "Forever," she says without missing a beat, hissing the word out in a hurried whisper. I look at her, scrunching up the space in between my eyebrows, and wonder if she realizes how absurd what she's just said is, but she will not turn to face me. "Forever is a long time," I say as I bend down, allowing her to climb onto my back.

I stand tall, shifting her weight on my hips, trying to find a spot where it feels comfortable. She is heavy, but not as heavy as I had expected. Sighing with each step, we move on. Her arms are wrapped around my neck, her breath hot in my ear and her presence slowly crushing me. I am quiet now, having run out of things to say to her, and preoccupied with the blisters that are forming on my heels, the dull ache in my spine, and the need to continue moving forward. Energized by the fact that she has now become even more burdensome to me, she busies herself by making up for my silence with useless words, a ceaseless monologue, ignoring the fact that I am ignoring her.

The longer I carry her, the heavier she becomes. Beneath her broken body, she is crushing my bones, my spirit. Approaching a crossroad, I drop her. The thud of her body hitting the ground sounds like twigs snapping and she looks up at me, too bewildered to speak at first. The sun dipping towards the horizon casts a red shadow over her, accentuating her boniness and her fragility. "What are you doing?" she demands, leaning on her hands, bruised legs stretched out before her. "I'm leaving you here," I tell her, looking over the top of her head. "We are done," I say. She lets out a heavy sigh. "No we're not," she says, screwing her face into an ugly frown. I have already begun going through our things, dividing what is mine from what is hers. "You can't leave me here," she argues. I look at her, scrutinizing her every feature. Her hair is greasy and plastered across her scalp, her cheeks hollow, and her dark eyes are ringed with neglect. She opens her mouth again to make noises of protest and I see that her smile has rotted away to expose swollen gums and a tongue that looks to have been cut with razor wire. "We are done," I repeat, cutting her off. She suddenly laughs, a forced burst and a halting sound, punctuated by her disdain for me. "You won't make it on your own, you know," she tells me. "You'll get lost," she says. "I will make my own map," I respond. "You're small. Too small. You're like a mouse; you're weak," she tells me, pouring her words over what is left of my spark, trying to extinguish it entirely. "I will become stronger," I say, turning my face, shutting my eyes against her voice. "What will people say?" she shouts, her words growing louder, fighting against the panic that is threatening to choke them out. "What will people say when they find out you that you left me?" she demands. "It will not matter," I tell her, "I will not hear them." She is screaming now, frustrated by anger, tears drawing lines through the dirt on her defeated face. "You are nothing without me," she hisses. "Nothing!" "Then I will make myself into something," I tell her and gather my belongings with my bearings.

I step back onto the road and look both ways. As I turn my back to the wave of insults she is throwing at me, I realize that I have been going the wrong way the whole time. I turn around and walk away. She is exhausting and I am exhausted. My movement, slow and painful at first, increases in speed with each passing mile and, as the sun of that first new day begins to rise, I turn around to make sure she has not followed me. She is leaning against a tree in the far off distance, head hanging down. She is the size of a pebble; her sound like the persistent buzz of an insect. I realize she is nothing. She is a disease. She is not me.

To give her a name would give her credit and clean now for ten years, the last time I turned to look for her, she was nowhere to be found.

Hard Lesson

Jim Martin

My name is Jim Martin and I have been active in the hardcore punk scene for decades. When I was a teenager back in the early 1980s, I decided to be a full-time hardcore punk. The time was right. I was a child of divorced parents and I was really pissed off and I guess I was acting out my rage. My parents were pretty creative and open-minded people. My folks never really restricted me from being a Punk. I guess as long as I did well in school, there was never really a problem with them. However, some of my friends had it pretty rough at home. Many of them would run away from home and end up at my house. I have two younger brothers and one more kid around the house never seemed to bother my mother. My friends would come over for a few days to cool off before eventually returning home.

My folks were pretty broke after their divorce. We lived in a poor neighborhood. My folks bought a "fixer upper" house that was always a work in progress. If my runaway friends were sitting around the house all day doing nothing, my stepfather Paul would put them to work sheet rocking, painting, or some other chore. At that time Paul was a therapist at The Yale Psychiatric Institute (Y.P.I.). He worked with teenagers at the Y.P.I. My mother was a trauma nurse at Yale New Haven Hospital.

The hardcore punk scene in New Haven was booming back in those days. Loads of gigs and many more new people were joining in on the scene. There would always be some new punk around town after a gig. Raybeez from Agnostic Front/Warzone stayed with us a few days, and I remember Danny, from Underdog, slept in his car in our driveway for a week. Many were runaways. If they were broke and hungry I would bring them back to my house to get something to eat. I guess that it was beginning to be a routine with me bringing people back to the house.

One time I brought home this new kid I just met, to get something to eat. We were sitting at the kitchen table when my stepdad came home. When he came in the back door, my friend said "Hello Paul." Paul looked pissed and went into the other room right away. I thought that this was weird. How did he know Paul? The kid wouldn't tell me. Paul asked me to come into the other room. Paul explained to me that this kid was his patient at Y.P.I. and had escaped. The police were looking for him. It was a complete coincidence that he had met me and I brought him home. Paul brought him back to Y.P.I.

That night we had a family discussion and I wasn't allowed to bring home strange kids anymore. I argued with my folks about this situation. I remember asking them what I was supposed to do when I met a new person, say "Hi, my name is Jim Martin. Are you nuts? If so, you can't come over to my house." I felt that my folks were being two-faced, but what it came down to was that it was their house and their rules. I moved out after that blowout. I eventually understood their position.

In the following years, I did meet more punks that escaped from Y.P.I., but I never turned them in. The punks who escaped were hospitalized by their parents because they were punks, and their parents were in shock and denial. I started to see it as a deprogramming of sorts. Sometimes Paul would call me and ask if I had seen any of his escaped patients. Then he realized and said to me, "You wouldn't tell me if you knew anyway." He was right. Kids don't rat on other kids. That was the rule. Some of the punks were throwaway kids from bad homes, but in time I did come to the realization that some were pretty depressed and sick. There was a rash of suicides in our scene. Was it teenage angst or clinical depression? I started to see the need for some professional help. My conflict was, am I maturing or selling out? It is definitely better help to keep your friends alive than having them die on you. I am profoundly sad and sorry to say that it took several deaths of my friends for me to realize that.

Living in the 1ˢᵗ Circle

Kristin Sarette

All I wanted was for the pain to stop. I just needed to find that place of serenity I found the first time I took a hit. I have not found it in a bottle or a bag since.

I was always searching for a solution but all I had were temporary answers to my permanent problem. I didn't know where to go.

All my friends had gone away one by one. My family had given up on me and my job couldn't keep me because I was a liability. I owed three months back rent and was being evicted. The world had opened itself up to me and I chose the path dimly lit and littered with the allure of dulling the pain of reality.

I had no idea where I was going and when I got to the end of the road I had cut myself to ribbons.

My hair was falling out of my head, my skin was green, and my innards were bleeding. My soul was like a mangled translucent sheet hanging by a thread. Every bag and drink ripping small holes until it was unidentifiable.

It's a funny thing; giving your soul away. It is the true definition of incomprehensible demoralization. I know this. I know this to the core of my very being. But there are other things I know.

I know there is hope. I know there is truth and I know there is a way out. The way out is through. How do you go through? How do you walk through pain with your corner stone in purgatory?

That is how I began to know truth and hope, built up from the dark seedy underbelly of self-affliction and hate. It is an experience no one should ever have to go through, but it happens every day.

The day I got sober was my day. I'd like to say I stayed sober but my path has been long and winding. Relapse after relapse landed me in a hell of my own making. My disease had a yellow light, looked both ways, and zoomed into ongoing traffic, crashing and burning into a pile of twisted burning wreckage. I finally became willing, willing to realize that I was worth it. That has made all the difference.

Through my life, especially through my recovery, recurring themes have enabled me to act a certain way or become who I wanted to be. They boil down to the unwritten rules of being an artist and the unspoken laws of living day-to-day life as a punk rock girl. The funny thing about these scenarios is that they do not exist.

This is why I chose the path less treaded. These two major components in my life require nothing of me but to be free and love myself. How amazing, a way to live is that? Any sort of expectations I put on these things or myself were purely out of fear.

When I finally hit the streets, after months of long-term chemical dependency treatment, I was armed with knowledge of my disease and a 12-step program. I was also in possession of something no one else had; I was the sole proprietor of my experience.

My experience has taught me many things. It has taught me that punk rock will NEVER let me down. It has taught me that my eyes can dilate to the sound of Stephen Egerton's guitar faster than they can with a bag. It has also taught me that I don't have to drink, fight, and fuck to fit into some fake image I created from years of warped thinking.

If there is one message I want to send it is this: It doesn't matter how you look, what you eat, what style of punk you listen to, what job you have, where you came from, or where you're going.

For me punk is none of these things. For me punk is a promise to myself to be true to my beliefs and to think outside the jar. Punk rock taught me to stand up for myself, give myself a chance and love me for me. Sobriety has taught me how to implement these beliefs in my day-to-day living and that has made all the difference.

Piece of $h!t at the Center of the Universe

Lyle Curry

I do not remember when I learned the definition of the term "alcohol- ism." But like many of us who experience these things first hand, I understood the meaning long before I picked up a dictionary. My first childhood memory is of my dad slamming the trunk of our old Buick on my thumb. It hurt like hell, but the main thing I remember is the fear. My mom was shaking and crying, saying "Is it broken Ragan, is it broken?" She was holding my hand in her palms. My limp little arm jumped around like a fish while she held it, and my dad tried to in- spect the wound but he was debilitated by guilt and indecision. When I got inside of our apartment, I stormed off to hide behind the recliner and cry. Lips pursed, arms suctioned tightly to my chest, this contin- ued to be the attitude with which I confronted emotional, mental, and physical pain and fear for many years to come.

It was an accident. Nothing my dad ever did to me included inten- tional physical violence. Was he drunk when he did it? That I would say, most likely so. Maybe he gushed about the incident at an A.A. meeting somewhere along the way, or maybe he kept it all inside. I'm betting on the latter. My parents' emotional make-up was very hot and cold. During my childhood and up until college, my mom treated me as a best friend rather than as her child. She was still a child herself really. She was thirty-one years old when I was born, but emotionally she was infantile. Even when I was young I knew she had very little grounding in reality. She was very religious, and put all of her trust in God—to the point where she would not take any initiatives in her life. To her it seemed that if it was meant to be, God would make it happen. She could not effectively address situations that came up in our lives. She shied away from decision-making and she couldn't express her needs and wants to people. This led to a bit of passive-aggressiveness, but on the whole she and I got along great and things were good for us. Her life would not start to fall apart until much later. As for how she related to me at that time, she smothered me in love and convinced me that I could do no wrong.

My father was an alcoholic living with schizotypal personality disorder. The term schizophrenia was the over-simplified, watered down word people used to talk about daddy's disease. It really gave no insight into what he actually suffered from. It wasn't until after he died that I learned there was a more exact term for his illness, and I think it was also referred to in his later years as schizoaffective disorder because of its progression. He was a seriously anti-social man. He lost job after job due to confrontations with co-workers and inability to co-operate with others. He was institutionalized at least five or six times for threatening public officials, and for challenging the authority of cops while drunk. The mental health system of Alabama failed him again, and again, and again, and he lashed out at them with vigor! As his alcoholism progressed alongside the mental illness, he withdrew more and more. He isolated himself to the extreme. In my early teens there were more outward signs of mental unrest, like delusional thoughts and manic-depression. He once made a threat to kill the governor while he was on-line in a chat room (this was the early '90s), for which the cops promptly showed up at our doorstep and ushered him away. He wrote scathing letters to public officials about people who worked in the mental health administration, and about policemen who had harassed him and treated him unjustly. All these things that happened never translated into better health care for my dad who was very clearly mentally unwell, it just translated into more and more visits to the sanitariums and more and more despondency and delusions. People just dismissed him as "crazy" and a hopeless alcoholic; quite a double whammy, don't you think?

I think daddy had believed at one point that he could find respite from his illness by securing a wife and a child in his life. But when that didn't work, and as I got older, his disease got worse. I realized even as a young teen that he was slowly becoming more and more incapable of relating to anyone. As a teenager, I tried so hard to engage him so that he might show me a little interest. But most of the time, he was not there. His physical body would be right next to me, but he was not present at all. I know that in addition to his mental problems he was drinking until black-out nearly every day, usually starting early and going until late. I also know that because of this lifestyle it must have been nearly impossible for doctors to get an accurate diagnosis for him.

My whole family was always trying to help him, to cure him; we begged him numerous times to put down the drink. He tried A.A. and I had heard rumors that my mom had been to Alanon. I did not hit my first Alanon meeting until this year, at twenty-eight years old. I definitely could have benefited from Alanon as a young adult; maybe my life would have been different had I gone. My mom and I were so busy trying to take care of my dad that we were not caring for ourselves; a problem that I know today is called co-dependency and it afflicts many family members of addicts and alcoholics.

To add insult to injury for me, things took a turn for the worse with my mom during my second year of college. Suddenly, she wasn't herself. She was asking people very pointed questions, and no one had any idea what she was talking about. For the first time in her life, she seemed to have an agenda. She was acting strong-willed, opinionated, and extremely loquacious. It was a very unnatural persona for her. I traveled home for spring break that year and I found that the woman who stood in front of me was no longer my mom. She looked like a ghost of my mother. The one thing that was physically different about her was a certain pallor to her skin. It almost looked transparent. The rest of her transformation was completely psychological. Her face and body language were so tense, aggressive, and manic. Nothing like the good-natured, light-hearted woman she had always been before. During the week that I was home I saw how sneaky and manipulative she was being towards others, and how extremely paranoid and delusional her thoughts were becoming. It was so alarming that once I returned to school I started planning a trip back home. I was terrified for her safety. She was going out at night to clubs, by herself, seeking out male attention with her scandalous outfits and public drunkenness. My mother had never been a drinker. But here she was, stumbling home at night drunk and alone, or with someone she did not know. She's lucky to be alive today!

Things exploded for us like a time bomb. It turned out mom was exhibiting the symptoms of bipolar I disorder, the most extreme form of all the bipolar spectrum disorders. Because of its long, slow build up for her, it erupted in a mania that was wild and violent, and mixed with many paranoid delusions. My grandmother and I bore the brunt of her attacks. She assaulted my grandmother once by pushing her down while they stood on the front steps of my grandmother's house. Her attacks at me were not physical because we were no longer in the same physical space; she attacked me with her insidious phone calls while I was at school. They ranged from vicious and cruel verbal assaults, to threats of suicide and disownment, to inconsolable sadness. She called at least four to six times every single day for at least two months. The issues of co-dependency had never been resolved for me, so I continued the cycle of trying to fix my mom like I had tried to do with my dad. Whats even more, I had been trying to fix mom for years because there were things that were happening in our home when I was in high school that I knew weren't right. It turned out those were the early signs of the bipolar disorder. That year it became nearly impossible for me to lead a normal life.

These were my parents, and I was their only child. My four grandparents also played a significant role in my upbringing. These family dynamics planted the seed of an internal war inside me about who I was and where I fit in to world. Was I the center of the universe? It was a concept that my mom and grandparents had instilled in me as a child. I was rarely scolded and I always got my way. In a word, I was spoiled. However, due to all the emotional trauma I endured, I also felt like a complete piece of shit. Was I just some lowly creature who couldn't even inspire her own father to love her? Someone who couldn't even help her mom loosen the grip of this strange and horrible illness? As a young person, these feelings of self-obsession and remorse dominated my subconscious. The discord they created led me down a ten plus year path of co-dependency, sex and love addiction, drug addiction, alcoholism, and mental instability.

My self-imposed isolation started alongside the earliest years of my sexuality. When I was seven, I started masturbating. I had this life-size stuffed Easter bunny that I kept in my bed with me throughout my second- and third-grade years in elementary school. After school each day, I would come home and get in bed with that bunny, and I would rub myself against it until I had an orgasm. I guess masturbation was my first experience with getting high. I was isolating myself from my friends (which hurt emotionally) with the sole intention of getting physical pleasure and a release from reality. I remember my mom would knock on the door to check on me and I would tell her I was just taking an afternoon nap. That excuse seemed viable enough to her, so she let me be.

My childhood was clearly turbulent; there were no boundaries, there were no authorities in the household, there were no rules. No one seemed to care what I did or when I did it. We moved around so much, I felt like a complete transient. My dad owned guns throughout my young adult life, and when we lived with him he would get drunk and play with them. Our home was never free from fear. My biggest setback was that I lacked insight into what a "normal" life might be like. There was no way for me to know what might bring sustainable happiness in my life, so I turned to quick fixes: boys, drugs, and alcohol.

I quickly became a drug addict. Marijuana was my drug of choice, even though it gave me paranoia. Then came the alcohol, then came the hard drugs. I was addicted to anxiety medicine: Klonopin and Xanax specifically; and prescription pain medication: Vicodin, Oxycontin, Morphine, Percocet, and Fentanyl. As a result of my progressing addiction, my mental state began to mimic my mom's bipolar disorder. I was on a manic high one moment, and having suicidal thoughts the next. I was attached at the hip to some boyfriend or lover one moment, and happily single the next. I was diagnosed as cyclothymic but, as with my dad, they could never get an accurate diagnosis for me because I was not sober. I was also diagnosed as having panic disorder. For my mood swings I was prescribed anti-psychotics, anti-anxieties, anti-convulsants, and anti-depressants. During this time period nothing seemed to work. I was so reprehensible! Couldn't they just prescribe an anti-me? I hated myself so much.

I spent ten years, from the age of seventeen to twenty-seven, living in my psychosis. I was self-deprecating, extremely self-centered, and completely terrified of everything. Nothing could curb my hunger for instant gratification, and at the same time nothing could fulfill me; nothing was ever enough. The two things that became truly intolerable for me were my panic disorder issues and my failing physical health. I was constantly afraid. Nothing except a high dose of pills and alcohol could take away this trench coat of fear that suffocated me every day. I had terrible asthma, to the point where I had constant shortness of breath and phlem. I always felt like I was suffocating; for years I felt that way. Between the breathing problems and the anxiety I could not function normally. Slowly, I started to acknowledge that there were some serious problems with my lifestyle. I started attending A.A. meetings, only to give up on the program in a few weeks time and relapse a few months later. This happened to me on several different occasions.

During these early stages of thinking about sobriety, my father died. He had been so profoundly affected by his alcoholism, that he was dealing with disastrous neurological damage and cirrhosis of the liver. He decided to step in front of a train on April 30, 2009. I wish I could say I stopped drinking and using after he died, but I still had another two-and-a-half years left before I found my way out. Substance abuse for me was tragic and life-threatening. I had no dignity left, and no awareness of the fact that there might be a life waiting for me out there without so much panic and anxiety. I finally made a decision to quit hard drugs about six months before I made the commitment to get completely sober. I thought maybe I could still drink and smoke pot and I would still get better. Finally I found that, for me, complete sobriety was the only answer. My last drink and drug were on December 3, 2011.

Since that day my world has truly opened up. As I write this, I have been sober for a year and a half. Today, I finally have freedom from that debilitating fear that I had lived with my whole life. I wake up every day grateful for what I have: a home, a job, a life, and most importantly, a loving group of people around me that I chose to call my family here in Queens, New York. My mom and grandmother still live in Alabama, where I grew up. I talk to them on the phone about once a week. I have a relationship with them, but it is formative one. They are both mentally unwell, but all I can do is show up for them in whatever ways that I can. I can be present for them today, but I certainly can't fix them! It is still frustrating to see them saying and doing the things that they say and do, and I know that they are probably never going to get it. But I can not change that. I can be a loving daughter and granddaughter without needing to save them from themselves. This subject really deals with the idea of acceptance, and accepting others as they are. I struggle with it, but I find that if I can't accept them for who they are, it is me who suffers in the end. I become angry, resentful, and discontented.

So, today, I try to have some peace and dignity in my life. I do not need someone else to fulfill me; I have myself. I don't need a drug or a drink to combat my sadness or anxiety; I am learning to sit through those feelings because feelings do pass eventually. I take care of myself today, and I trust myself to deal with the things that come.

I have found that I can control my anxiety, naturally, as long as I stay healthy and sober. Not everyone can do that; some people need medication and there is absolutely nothing shameful about needing help. It does not make you a failure, it does not make you less of a man, woman, punk, career person, athlete, artist, writer etc., etc., etc. I personally have found that I can use my own forms of medicine everyday to keep me half-way sane: exercise, acupuncture, meditation, service to others, and fellowship. These things help me to deal with life and its challenges. I am very protective of my sanity and of my sobriety. If someone or something is becoming a threat to my well-being, I have to separate myself from him, her, or it.

It is my opinion that everyone needs a program. And, for those who suffer from addiction and/or mental health issues, we especially need a program of recovery. As people who suffer from the disease of mental imbalance, we have to take more action than others do in order to stay healthy. We have to do more work each day to be well. Sometimes finding a structured program helps to make our lives manageable again. But I do not advocate any one particular path to recovery. I believe it is everyone's own decision what method they will use to stay healthy, and if need be, to sober up, both literally and figuratively.

My personal wellness really pivots on how well I take care of myself every single day. I know now that I am not the piece of shit that I once thought I was. I was always deserving of a father's love and affection. I was always deserving of a family that had stability and safety, but things didn't happen for me that way. And I am also not the center of the universe. Other people have feelings, needs, wants, desires, and insecurities. My feelings and reactions are not omnipotent. I have to constantly check that self-centeredness at the door. Doing service for others really helps me with that. I have people who love me and to whom I feel accountable. They deserve to be treated with respect, just as I will always demand respect from them. I must take an active role in my life in order to be a worker among workers, and a contributing member of the family that I love and trust. In other words, I am neither a piece of shit, nor the center of the universe, and gratefully so.

Been Down So Long That It Seems Like Up To Me (Travis Cut)

Mac

My name is Mac . . . and I am a manic depressive.

There it is. In black & white. For all to see.

In spite of a diagnosis in my tender hormone-fuelled teenage years, it took another twenty years before I "came out" publicly about my depression. And by that time a lot of damage had been done.

The teenage boy that went into hospital, unconscious, after fist-fuls of paracetamol washed down with vodka, died that night, and it was "Mac" that came "round." But that's not where the story began.

I always knew there was something wrong with me, from a very early age. Even though I didn't really have any understanding, it wasn't "normal" for the police to turn up because a five year old had delib-erately destroyed a field of corn and hurled abuse at the farmer, was it? Not quite "right" that that same five year old was slippered by the headmaster on his second day at school for the crime of "leading a revolt" and taking half the class of (probably crying) toddlers out of the school gates on the first day with a motivating speech of "Let's go home"?

The signs were there that things were "damaged" inside my head, but amongst the few things that seemed to inspire me, calm me, bring me any joy, was music. It had always played a part in my life, with my father being in bands, playing all over, filling the house with assorted noise. Blues, jazz, classical, rock. I learned piano, I learned to play trombone (pretty well too) I learned to read and write music. I fell in love with '50s rockabilly—the style, the music, and the rebelliousness.

And just like every other misfit, loser, and fuck-up I suddenly discovered punk rock. It was about me, damnit! I'd fallen in love with someone I shouldn't have fallen in love with. Yep, I'd asked myself "What's My Name?" I was "In A Rut." Arguably, I was probably an "Orgasm Addict" around that time too. But that's another story altogether.

Then it happened. I raided the drinks cabinet, nicked the vodka, popped a load of pills, and turned the volume up on a hometaped compilation of the songs I loved—the Clash, Ruts, Stray Cats, Blondie—and went to sleep.

A few months in a hospital followed, filling the days with a cassette player, making compilation tapes from the John Peel Show, and following a shrink's advice to make a list of things I wanted to achieve in my life to help me believe there was a reason to carry on. How could either of us have known that before I was thirty I was somehow going to be lucky enough to have achieved them all already?

Music and misery always fit perfectly together, but it was the *music* that drove me forward. I lied about my age to join bands, I lived to play music, it was an all-consuming passion—to lead a completely rock'n'roll lifestyle with all the hedonism but none of the rockstar arrogance. I bought into the "live fast, die young, leave a pretty corpse" ideal 100 percent.

I was regularly playing in pubs (drinking and smoking quite heavily) with jazz bands at fifteen; engaged at seventeen; touring Europe by nineteen; a tour of East Germany before the Berlin Wall came down at twenty; joining the growing collection of 7" and 12" slabs of noise that I cherished were some with my name on them.

And I was loving it; every cold, uncomfortable second crammed in the back of a transit van was just as exciting and fulfilling to me as every second of seeing people bouncing around to the noise I was making onstage. There were stints with The Neurotics, The Pharaohs,

The Internationalists, Amino & The Acids, Blue Summer, The Pillage People, The Cougars, and failed attempts at forming my own bands, like Clare Grogan's Scar and The Atoms. Even though it was clear to anyone I was a "psychobilly," to me genre was irrelevant. I knew what I loved, and I was going to play it—punk rock, rockabilly, reggae, power pop, or trad jazz. I was having the time of my life!

Or so it appeared . . . to anyone that wasn't in my head, that is.

I would lock myself away in whatever shared house, flat, or squat I was living in, and involuntarily wallow in utter self-loathing. I had no idea why, there was (and still is) no reason for it, but I often found myself crying, alone, listening to loud music.

Where the drugs and alcohol in public were just the hedonistic life-style being played out as a display of how great everything was, few, if any, could see that it was nothing more than over-compensating for the misery and loneliness that lurked just below the surface. It was harder to isolate myself then, promoting a venue full time, playing, touring, recording, so I just had to surround myself with people who wouldn't see that, even in a crowd, I was alone and even with a smile, I was crying.

When the black cloud descended, and it did with alarming regularity, still does, I self-medicated. I drowned the "black dog" with alcohol, and killed the pain with drugs, and this slowly became a solo activity as well a public one. In private there was no pretense—it was about coping with the torment whilst harming myself as much as I could. The "live fast" part of the equation was there for all to see (and I'll admit it made me feel a little proud), but the "die young" part was kept behind closed doors. And just looking at the old photos anyone can see the "leave a pretty corpse" part was never an option anyway.

I was conducting my own not-so-controlled "experiments" on the effects of acid on depression, I was probably stoned to some degree every day, I would keep myself up for days at a time because I was a fiend for speed in any form, and I started injecting. Not a very sociable way to get out of your head at the best of times. One of the lowest points I can recall, was holding my bare arm straight out behind me, tourniquet in place, begging someone to inject me—my first hit. I wasn't a fan of needles, but I wanted to know what it felt like. Would it be my savior? A miracle cure? Or maybe it would end my pain in another way? Either way it was a win/win for me. Well done me, I managed to "lose" a win/win game. After the all-too-short-lived releases from my own dark thoughts, I was left with less money, in debt to some pretty nasty characters, and with a new guilt to add to the despair I felt on a semi-permanent basis.

And there were numerous occasions when I returned to the familiar routine of throwing painkillers and vodka down my neck and ending up in hospital. I was sectioned, I was pumped full of antidepressants, I was talked at, but I didn't want anyone to know. So the "public persona" was all I could let out in the world while all the real feelings stayed in me. Even girlfriends, fiancés, lovers, and a wife weren't allowed to see the painful truth, not that they would have wanted to. That reality wasn't what they signed up for after all.

All that time songs poured out of me, most of them were naïve, poorly crafted garbage, blatantly ripping off my favorite bands to accompany the pitiful whining I called "lyrics." But with practice, songs I felt happy with started to appear. I'd read the *Maximum Rock 'n' Roll Guide to Write Your Own Bad Religion Song!* All I needed was a band, so one day in '93, Travis Cut were formed.

Finally I was able to write punk rock songs that acted as a form of therapy, and that were enjoyed by others. Every song I wrote (and still write) is personal, every one a true story of the (nearly always) dark thoughts and experiences that I knew all too well, but couldn't bring myself to admit in public.

I spent months homeless after separating from my wife, but it gave me the song "Mailage" full of bitter resignation over the way the prolonged divorce played out.

"In Vain" was, quite explicitly, about the times I was injecting.

"Acceptance" was a suicide note set to music.

It would hurt when someone would write to the band and say that one of my songs really meant something to them, or they related to it. Whilst I was seriously flattered that something I'd written meant enough to them for them to put pen to paper, it tore me apart to think that anyone was going through the personal torment that I was, or that I had suffered to write that particular lyric. Occasionally I got angry, shouting "NO YOU DON'T! YOU HAVE NO IDEA WHAT I WAS LIVING THROUGH! HOW COULD YOU!" at someone's letter, before the guilt, the shame, and the self-loathing took over. Was their pain my fault, or the fault of my lyric? Did I put them in touch with some feeling or emotion that had hurt them? I hated the thought that anyone was suffering the things I was. But other than through songs and lyrics, I still couldn't let people know what was actually going on, that I was on anti-depressants, or that I was in and out of different courses of therapy and counseling. I masked it all with musical endeavors, both my own and that of others by putting on show after show, band after band—"Mac" had already become "Mac From the Square."

I had, by this time, come to the conclusion that anything that brought me happiness was nothing more than a cover over the murky and frightening reality. When that cover was taken away, I was left confronting the festering pile of neuroses that made up my emotional wreckage. Never was that more true than when the "cover" I'd been using was a relationship. And I couldn't cope with the rejection. The mask I wore had started to occasionally crack and let the true desperate depressive show through, and that made me hate myself even more. Of the many "black cloud" episodes, and overdoses, the vast majority were never publicly known about, but some were. Often triggered by relationship breakdowns, or by being thrown out of a band, the bad times became increasingly public.

Remember the list written by the "newborn" Mac? Well, the Travis Cut Japan tour and recording an album in the US were the final ones to tick off. A list of things, I thought were totally infeasible, had been completed and I drifted into a period of mentally treading water. Music continued to be the be all and end all, but I had also fallen in love with someone who was my "rock" (to use a well-worn cliché). The extremes had gone from my life though, extremes that kept me alive. I no longer had any ambitions left, and the despair and isolation crept back in. I started to be a little more honest about my condition, I had, after all, been suffering with it for many many years.

My "rock" finally walked away after seven amazing years, leaving me in the city I had made my home just to be with her. But she had no choice, my depression had taken it's toll on both of us and she needed to refresh and start anew. This triggered the start of my worst (and still current) episode, only this time I had no reason to hide it. I had already let that side of me be seen by people around me. As I sank lower and lower, my behavior became more unacceptable, my drinking and substance use became out of control, and because of it, I was thrown out of the band I was playing in. People I thought of as good friends distanced themselves or, in many cases, turned their backs. I became isolated, vulnerable, and scared. Suicide attempts and plans, too numerous to count, seemed almost daily. Although in reality, they were probably less often, but the attempts were much more determined than before. Every song I heard, lyric I wrote, or TV show I saw sent me the message that I was worthless, that there was no point anymore. Every knock on the door and every ringing telephone, sent me into a spiral of panic attacks, inexplicable guilt, and reasonless tears. I lost all self control.

I sat at a computer and told the world what I was and how I felt. The act of writing it down didn't give me the release I was hoping for, but just clicking a button that suddenly sent those words out into the public domain did. In some way, it was like "cyber self-harm"—making myself vulnerable and in pain by opening up my heart and soul to an army of strangers who had no reason to care. My inner turmoil was laid bare. All the covers had *been* wrenched from the rotting waste that was my chaotic mental state. The repeated abuse through overdoses, alcohol, drugs, and rock'n'roll lifestyle had actually left me physically damaged as well as mentally. No turning back.

I have clawed some of my self-esteem back, still playing shows, and still managing to paint on the mask to go out and socialize. Now, people are more aware that I am severely ill. So, I don't feel the same guilt if I have to slip quietly away and go home, or if I just can't make it out of my front door.

There is still a long way to go, the story is far from over. I still suffer from the lowest lows, coupled with guilt about it because I have no right to feel like this.

I've over-run the word count, it's early hours of the morning, I'm out of weed, my coffee's cold, and I have a doctor's appointment in a couple of hours. It seems that of the three things that have defined me—punk rock, depression, and a quiff—only my hair is diminishing.

This is the most painfully personal thing I've ever written that didn't have a guitar riff!

My Drunken Years Of Hell

Maija Sarkkama

Yes, I would say I'm crazy!

My life used to be a hell-of-a-lot crazier due to my alcohol addiction, which I battled for about fifteen years. I'm almost thirty-three years old now. I am originally from Finland, but I moved to Edinburgh, Scotland, when I was eighteen years old after finishing high school. I wanted to get away and start a new life abroad. Obviously, at that age, it was great to be away from my family. They couldn't keep an eye on me and I could do whatever the hell I wanted.

I had been drinking, quite heavily, even before I moved away. When I moved to Edinburgh, it was a big party all the time. I could drink as much as I wanted without anybody controlling me. I started experimenting with drugs as well. I got involved with the local punk scene and started my first band in 2000 with my then-boyfriend and a couple of friends. I was the singer. It was a garage/riot grrl punk band called Miuku and we managed to play together for nearly four years.

By that time my drinking was out of control. I would get too wasted before band practices, which obviously caused a few problems. Most gigs I managed to do OK but I would always have a bit too much to drink. I would get hammered when I went to see other bands and not really remember much of it the next day. Then there was the shame of making a fool out of myself but I would just carry on the same way. I had no desire to cut down and there was the stereotypical thing about the punk scene; people get wasted. It was just a part of it, the "Drunk Punx" thing.

Around 2004, my parents started getting really worried about me. Whenever they called I would be drunk and they could hear that in my voice. Also, sometimes I didn't answer the phone for weeks. l was too wasted to talk and that added to their worry. I wonder how I managed to complete a degree in sociology and psychology at the university. I wasn't even trying to get a job related to my degree. I was more interested in drinking. So, I did simple temp work like housekeeping or working in pubs. I got fired from several jobs because I would come to work too hungover or not turn up at all. For a couple of years, I was on social security benefits.

I had suffered from depression since 2000 and was put on antidepressants. They didn't really work with the amount I was drinking. Alcohol is a depressant. I guess, my drinking just made it worse but I didn't realize that and just kept drinking more and more to take my mind off it.

My parents started blaming my punk rock lifestyle and the people I was hanging out with for my problems but, clearly, that was not the case. The problem was I was addicted to alcohol, full stop.

In 2006, I tried to get my act together and did a year-long course in holistic therapies, as I had an interest in that, and I thought it would help to keep my drinking under control. I did cut down a little and managed to get qualifications in reflexology and aromatherapy but as soon as my course ended, my drinking was back. I started a new band with my ex-boyfriend, an anarcho, hardcore-punk band called Down to Kill. Even in those days, our gigs with DTK were pretty successful and I really tried to put more effort into it. I really enjoyed it and wanted to take it more seriously but I would still turn up at practices way too drunk or miss practices because of my drinking. We carried on and a lot of people really got into our music.

At the time, I was trying to work as a self-employed holistic massage therapist but that didn't really work out too well because of the amount I was drinking. I went back on social security and my purpose in life was to drink and sing in a band. Career-wise things were pretty much at a dead end.

Every time I went to visit my family back in Finland, I tried to put on an act that I was doing OK even though I wasn't. I visited them twice a year and they tried to help me with psychotherapists, hypnotherapists, and alcohol counselors but they didn't help at all. I wasn't willing to stop drinking. I did want to get it under control but nothing worked.

A few times, I went to a self-help group for women with alcohol problems. My doctor referred me to the Alcohol Problems Clinic. My liver tests were showing signs of liver disease but even that couldn't stop me. I got a little worried and cut down for a couple of months, but just until my next blood test. The results were better and so I thought, "Well, that's great, I can drink loads again!"

My drinking was affecting me in every way; physically and mentally. After two-week benders I would feel like I was going to die. I would shake, sweat, hallucinate, and constantly throw up. My mind was full of paranoia, guilt, and confusion. I was scared to leave the house and scared of seeing anybody apart from my boyfriend; he was as bad as me with the drink.

I would tell myself "never again," but it would just happen again and again. I wasn't even enjoying drinking anymore; I just had to have it, even if I didn't really want it.

In 2009, I tried to get a grip of myself by getting a full-time job at a pharmacy. I managed to cut down a bit since I had to be there Monday through Friday. I would still turn up hungover and fuck knows how I got away with it. My colleagues could tell I was having problems with alcohol but they never had a serious discussion with me about it. I would phone in sick quite often and be off for a week or two; always giving excuses and that's when I started getting warnings from my boss.

The warning bells really started ringing for me when I was missing my favorite bands' gigs because of alcohol. Then in March, 2010 I saw my rock bottom. I had been drinking 24/7 for over two weeks and was in one hell of a state. I lived on my own. My boyfriend had found me unconscious on the floor, foaming at the mouth. I had been mixing sleeping pills with alcohol, not to kill myself, but to numb myself.

When he woke me up I started screaming like hell and the neighbors phoned the police. I was so wasted I couldn't even speak to the cops when they questioned me. I was taken to the hospital kicking and screaming.

I sobered up a little in the hospital and tried to escape, to get more booze. The hospital staff eventually let me go because I was getting aggressive and demanding. I was only wearing a nightgown and didn't have any money or my keys. I managed to get a taxi (which I never paid for) to my boyfriend's apartment. I hadn't realized he was still at mine and waiting to hear from me. His neighbor let me in. By coincidence, he was a heavy drinker and had loads of booze in the house. He didn't know anything about me but let me stay.

I drank all of his booze and the next morning he got angry at me. He didn't know who the hell I was. He thought I just turned up in the middle of the night and stole all of his booze. He called the cops and they took me back to the hospital in handcuffs. I was VERY lucky that this guy was a decent person; otherwise anything could have happened to me that night.

I was totally wasted when the cops questioned me at the hospital, but I explained I had serious drinking problems. After many hours they took me back to my place. My boyfriend and two good friends were waiting for me.

Anyway, my boyfriend had told my mum that I had been taken to the hospital and her and my dad took the first available flight to Edinburgh. When they saw me they both started crying because I looked like an absolute wreck. I will remember that night for the rest of my life. I thought I was going to die, for real.

The withdrawal symptoms were indescribable. I was screaming with pain, shaking like hell, sweating bucket loads and my heart was beating very irregularly. My mum was lying next to me, trying to cool me down by waving a piece of paper. It really felt like a miracle that I survived that night. The next day, when I had sobered up a bit, we had a serious discussion and I finally admitted that I needed help, badly. I had to go to rehab. The waiting lists in Scotland can be three–four months so my parents insisted that I go to Finland with them and get treatment there. I think if they'd left my by myself I probably would have died in a couple of months.

I went to Finland with my parents and got into rehab within two weeks. It was a treatment center for both alcoholics and drug addicts, but female only. I was nervous as hell going there, but it was the best thing I've ever done. It saved my life. I stayed there for a month, which is the standard treatment period. While I was there, I got a letter from my work offering me a second chance. I could have stayed there even longer, but I decided to take this chance and returned to Edinburgh.

While I was in the rehab, I got introduced to a 12-Step Program and as soon as I returned to Edinburgh, I started going to local meetings every week. It is nothing like I imagined it to be. It's not about preaching about God or being serious all the time. I have met great people and we have great laughs as well! It gives me so much support. It's wonderful to share your experiences with people who really understand and have been through the same shit.

I have now been alcohol free for over two years and it just seems like a miracle. Everybody keeps telling me how much I have changed, for the better. Physically and mentally I feel a million times better. I now enjoy singing in Down to Kill even more. I can perform a lot better and remembering our gigs is great! First, it was really hard going to gigs sober, when almost everyone else is drinking, but it doesn't bother me anymore. I have no cravings for alcohol. I know that if I took one drink, it would go straight back to that hell and I never want to go there again. I want to help other alcoholics as much as I can but I have realized that you have to want it. You cannot force anyone into it. I also feel like a much stronger person having gone through all this and I have learned to appreciate life a lot more. I take it one day at a time and I'm grateful for every single day. It feels like such a gift to still be alive.

Satori by a Soul Citizen

Marika Ley a.k.a. Marika Provokator, Misc. Mari, Terroreza

"**D**o these people know who I am and what I've done? That I was a junkie and a criminally minded, whore? Nope! They haven't a clue, and it doesn't matter one iota at this moment! I never anticipated this."

The point of satori,[1] that I could be considered a sane citizen, came when I received my first sponsorship money upon the acceptance of my first proposal for said monetary sponsorship. I was late for the meeting and my best attempt at business attire was falling apart—literally at the seams. My boots, the sole of which decided to leave my second hand ensemble, separating and flopping about like a dead fish, caused me to walk with an exaggerated step resembling the

---

1 Satori (悟り?) (Chinese: 悟; pinyin: wù; Korean 오; Vietnamese ngộ) is a Japanese Buddhist term for enlightenment, meaning "understanding". In the Zen Buddhist tradition, satori refers to the experience of kensho.[1] Kensho (Japanese) is a term used in Zen traditions meaning "seeing into one's true nature." Ken means "seeing," sho means "nature," "essence."[1] Satori and kensho are commonly translated as enlightenment.

gait of party clown with only one oversized shoe (the Minister of the Ministry of Silly Walks mid-mishap).

I was afraid I would be discovered as a fraud at some point and the awarded funds for the proposed project, a DIY anti-film festival in Praha, would be rescinded once the sponsors, a high-end international bank, realized that I was who I was.

This totally blew my mind. All they knew was that I was an entrepreneur of sub-culture film productions, something I myself had only recently become aware that I was. They didn't know about the robberies, the prostitution, or the long history of mental instability and hospital visits. In fact it wasn't until they met me in person did they realize I wasn't the clientele they are accustomed to.

I didn't win the award with my attire or nice, neat, pink haired biz-bun; it was my intellect, logic and reasonable request for support. Perhaps it was the first and most important validation I could ever receive. It bolstered my long-held belief that I am not crazy or sick.

All of my life, and to this day I never felt sick or crazy but attuned and eerily enlightened, like a clairvoyant or a shaman. Buttressed by the whacked-out reactions of everyone around me, I honestly feel I am among the few who are sane. In hindsight, it was the honesty that earned me the moniker of "sick pup." If I was asked my opinion, I said it. Often, I spoke my mind even if I wasn't asked. If it felt like an injustice I reacted, regardless of rules and expectations of situations specific social norms. I would and still can get physically sick to my stomach if I don't address an injustice I might of just witnessed. Yes, I heard voices and they were/are my conscience. At times they were/are guardian angels and at other times reckless instigators but they were always honest. At these times the voices would be instigating me to honor my gut, *"If you don't do something or say something you'll regret it for a long time. Maybe if you do something now this injustice will be less likely to occur in the future . . . and that's up to you!"* (mind you I am addressing myself in my own head).

BE FOREWARNED: The following is the me I know that is constantly a subtext to the me you see (before you):

Survivalist tactics to endure the hardships of the sensitive soul, are often the psychiatry's checklist for the sick psyche, but who the fuck are they to judge me or you? Why, if I am really "sick," am I doomed to stay that way? S-I-C-K stamped on the head for all to see as I stumble from one insipid scenario to another. Why can I not get better? Or get better at being SICK? If I must settle for the SICK psychiatric stamp, for mental aberrations or addictive inclinations, couldn't I learn how to be SICK in society and not be sorry about it? Isn't that infinitely better than being stuck being sad?

The sense of being "found out" as fraudulent fades once one is at peace with the sickness of sensitivity. If your actions and opinions are sincere, then what is SICK? In my opinion, more people need to be this sort of SICK in our society, or at the very least honor its worth.

Sure there are certain things, as an existing citizen, I cannot do without disrupting the lives of others. Now that I am fully aware of the consequences of my actions, I must choose to exercise my prowess in the following areas with caution and reserve;

Public Inebriation: I can't shoot up (with syringes), at least not until I'm ninety years old and no one gives a shit anymore. Heroin is a bad idea as a habit. As history has taught me it always turns into a habit and is a handy hole to hide in. But in effect any substance used to quell the heart, soul, and mind has in it the ability to dampen all aspects of sentience. Communication is key, and although the village idiot is oddly enough forgiven for murmuring misanthropic missives . . . equally no one will really pay attention unless in hindsight.

Rebellious Liberation: there is a romantic draw to the illegal action. Outside of Robin Hood-like reasoning, robbery, vandalism, protest, random art, etc. . . . is bad behavior and listening to the voices that instigate abnormally intense actions aren't always my angels. This is another thing I'll allow when I'm ninety (doing anything I fuckin' want to, just because I feel it is relevant to the moment). I do this now but to a much tempered degree, in order to stay out of institutional incarceration.

Unbridled Honesty: among the many positives of having all your senses be super acute, is the negative of being aware of something(s) that most people aren't. It is either they are not sensitive to whatever the aberration is or that they are in denial of it. If you, as the seer, call it out by name . . . whatever it is, be prepared to be ostracized for seeing it and saying it out loud thereby making it "real" or known.

Its saddens one to realize that in order to relate (and be related to), one must always exercise a certain restraint in order to be heard. But that is the truth of the matter. If you want that one door you want to walk through to be opened—you can't let the gate keeper know that within your mind resides several personalities, or that you might have a few monkeys on your back when you pass over the threshold. Just smile and act normal (and don't say anything about the purple dinosaur on the ceiling).

All that being understood, what has this SICK punk done in spite of the "permanent" prognosis?

After the therapy of ibogainei and the awareness that is its potent push toward the awakening of the self and then learning how to steer that self (sort of like the scene of Bambi learning how to step), what have I done?

This sick chick moved to the Czech Republic, where she knew nothing of the culture let alone the language and started a magazine (not knowing how to publish periodicals), produced three film festivals, promoted countless concerts, and produced several music festivals. All run as a volunteer- and intern-manned organization that started several students in their current careers. I also sing in a band while slurring Czechoslovak sentences. I sing like a strung-out sycophant star because I never really stopped to learn Czech proper and just to piss people off I'll mix in some German too.

Sick . . .

Oddly enough . . . throughout all of that, over a decade of activities promoting art and creativity vis-à-vis the support structure of pointed proposal and propositions provided by the corporate community under the guise of cultural communication—actually the "Man" to pay money to produce DIY Film Festial that openly sought to benefit and suport a militant vegan organization that was also a watchdog group for Abuse of Animals of Labor. People of all walks of life, culture, creed, shapes, and sizes called me crazy (and that for doing things like art mags, fests and the like. I mean like, above ground sponsored stuff!). At that point . . . Fuck 'EM.

Me or the World?

Matt Hollander

I have suffered from depression for a long time. I can't remember exactly when it started, but even back in elementary school I remember having thoughts of depression. Being put on Ritalin for ADD at a young age definitely had an impact on my depression, and I believe changed me in some way.

It's hard to tell exactly where the depression comes from. One thought that always come to my mind, is it the world/society or is it me/my brain? The short answer is probably both nature and nurture affect depression. This is a question I have always wondered about—is it my brain or the world? Society is sick and backwards, and we are forced to deal with the symptoms not with what causes the problems. We strive for growth and the ultimate, not progress or sustainability. As a society we think about ourselves and not others. We blame the person, not the surroundings and the environment that makes the person. This is a problem and I have seen it as one of the many causes of depression.

We have been disconnected with the natural world. We have created and accepted these systems and institutions, and we believe that this is the only acceptable way to live. If you don't like it, live that way, or follow the societal rules, you are labeled crazy, weird, or wrong. This leads to depression and the disconnect to the real, natural world and what really matters! We are not allowed to live free. Free from fear, free from judgment of others. We only value the best and the normal, not the different and mediocre or even bad. This makes us hide from others and ourselves, and what we really feel and think. In turn, we lie to ourselves and others every day. This fear of being judged breeds self hate, and that leads to hurting others and yourself. We put on masks and barriers to protect ourselves, but in the end they hurt us and everyone around us. Self hate breeds hate.

We live in a crazy world. Sometimes living in a crazy world people do things that under "normal" situations some people wouldn't do. Someone having a sane reaction to a crazy situation, we then look back on the incident and we say the person is crazy, not society or what happened before the incident. Crazy isn't a fair word. People aren't crazy, they are misunderstood. Crazy is a dismissive word. You don't understand them so they must be crazy, but couldn't the environment be a little sick? Things are not always as they seem.

I have thoughts of depression, suicide, despair, discontent, and anxiety. These states aren't constant, they come and go in a vicious cycle. The cycle of depression goes back and forth, happy, sad, mad. They are just states of mind and change constantly. You can't feel happy unless some times you feel sad.

Depression is a block in your head, at the forefront of your brain and conscience, that won't let go. It's a visor between you and the world. Nothing will get in or out without going through the depression filter, until it wears off. Happiness fades in slowly and stealthily. Both happiness and depression are ever-constant changing states.

The depression block is an all-encompassing pressure, total and complete. Nothing else matters at that moment and almost nothing can change the feelings but time. The pain hits the core of your being and tells it no more, it's not worth it, the pressure is squashing my mind and I'm done. Depression makes your brain incapacitated. Other things don't matter. Your brain doesn't want to play the games of life anymore. Depression makes you lost and disillusioned with the world, people, relationships, goals, and even things you usually like. The weight is like you are wearing a giant down coat and it's drenched in water and you're too heavy to lift yourself out of the pool.

Society can't be changed in one day, but trying to be true to yourself and others is a good way to start and deal with depression. Other ways that have helped me with depression and anxiety are with exercising; cooking and eating a good balanced meal; creating art; music, writing, painting, drawing; reading; growing or building things; stretching; dancing; screaming; riding bikes; being in nature; and doing something you are scared to do. For me, when I do as many of these things in a day, it definitely helps my depression and mental well-being. Another tool that has helped my anxiety is meditation. There are many different types of meditation and different methods work for different people. I highly recommend trying out some forms of meditation and if they don't fit with you, don't give up. There are many styles to explore and the more you do it, the easier it gets and the more you will see results.

Depression is a long battle. It's something I think I will deal with for the rest of my life. Through these tools and through trying to live my life for today, to be here now, and be honest to myself and the people around me, I'll try and get through the days. Keep fighting fear and preconceived notions.

No Sleep, No Cures

Matt Svendsen

For twenty years I have suffered from mental illness. My ability to live a normal life is severely compromised because of this illness. It is not a coincidence that I have been devoted to punk as a counter-culture for that same period of time. The only moments I feel free from my problems at all are when I'm making music or involved with punk in some way.

This is about the reality disabled punks face on a daily basis. It's the reality I'm not allowed to share with people unless I feel like triggering a quick demise of my friendships. Mostly, I would like to cover my participation in the punk scene and how my disability affects my level of involvement.

I experienced a fair amount of trauma early in life. My mother was assaulted while I was in the womb and she barely survived. Her doctors told her I might be born with disabilities but she had me anyway. During my childhood, I had asthma. Because of the asthma, I was kept in the hospital inside a plastic bubble off and on through-out childhood. I grew up in the middle of nowhere (a farm in Eastern Montana). My social life was very isolated. I didn't have many friends, so I spent most of my time with my family. When I was fourteen, my mom was hit by a truck while crossing the street in a small town near our home. Once again, she barely pulled through and I had to move to Missoula to live with my dad. By this time, I was suffering from depression and social anxiety. This is also around the time that I discovered punk. Through punk, I finally felt like I had something I could belong to—a group of people who were like me: awkward, nerdy, antisocial, angry, frustrated, and fed up with society.

By the time I was eighteen, I had a full-blown panic disorder that was completely out of control. Even after being put on a constant supply of Lorazepam (and used as a guinea pig for every anti-depressant and anti-psychotic known to man), I still end up in the emergency room on a regular basis—often with a heart rate over 200 beats-per-minute. I usually try to make light of the situation by saying I have "the fastest heart in the west." But to be honest, every attack is terrifying. Every time it happens, I am convinced that I'm dying. I can feel my brain melt inside my head. I can feel electricity all over my body and my heart feels like it could explode at any minute.

During this time, my daughter Kieran was born. Despite my illness, I was able to develop my parenting skills and, to this day, I share equal custody of Kieran. Without her, I know that I would be dead. She has always been there for me. She is sixteen years old now and she is nothing less than a genius. She has made me a very proud parent and she will never know just how much I owe to her. I feel as though I have come a long way and much of it is thanks to her.

I immediately began seeing a psychiatrist every week and learned breathing exercises, Tai Chi, meditation, as well as other methods for relaxation to counter the constant anxiety. Still, I have found that the best therapy for me is playing music. In 1999, I started a band with some friends. This was an outlet for the frustrations we felt from living in a state where bigotry, sexism, racism, homophobia, and excessive consumerism were prevalent social customs. We were feminists and we were also anarchists. Ani Difranco happened to be playing a show in Missoula around the time we played our first show. We were joking about how sappy and annoying she was and the name for our band naturally became THE ANTI DIFRANCOS.

Among the social/political issues we concerned ourselves with in the band, there was one issue that I felt needed a little more attention:

straightedge. I became aware that the drugs and alcohol I had been using to self-medicate were actually contributing to my anxiety issues rather than helping them. I quit drinking and, in 2000, I started a straightedge band called VENAL I.V.

Neither of these bands was very "successful" in terms of being popular in the punk scene. We were living in the middle of nowhere and we were poor, so touring was difficult and rare. Still, these bands served a purpose for us and that's what mattered. We made DIY releases, booked shows for touring bands, and wrote fanzines. Around 2002, I decided to combine the various projects I was working on under one banner and POISONED CANDY RECORDS was born.

In 2002 both bands broke up and I was immediately asked to join a band from Kalispell called ASS-END OFFEND. I had known these guys for a while and THE ANTI DIFRANCOS had done a west coast tour with them the year before. I joined ASS-END OFFEND and noticed quickly that we all had the same ambitions. We did extensive touring all over the U.S. (three full U.S. tours and about a dozen west coast tours) as well as a trip to Eastern Europe. We learned a lot in the recording studios and were releasing new records frequently. Although I was really medicated, I was still able to function well enough to do these things and I got to see a lot of the world that I otherwise would never have had the opportunity to see.

In 2005, ASS-END OFFEND.temporarily broke up. One by one, all the band members moved to Portland, OR for different personal reasons. For me, serving twenty-seven years in the social penitentiary known as Montana was more than enough of a reason to escape, but my daughter's mom was also moving to Portland so it just made sense to make the move there myself. In 2006, we started playing together again under a new name, SQUALORA, and continued putting out records and touring.

About three years ago, I was asked to join a new Portland band, RAW NERVES, as the singer. I was really excited to be a part of this project. I got to write all of the lyrics and make some of the art, which was very therapeutic for me. I wrote a lot of political-themed material as well as personal stuff related to my disability. This band was also very motivated and I feel like we accomplished quite a lot.

Around the time I joined RAW NERVES, my symptoms became much worse and I began to develop new illnesses—psychosis and dissociative amnesia. When diagnosed with a mental illness, not only do people distrust your judgment, they oftentimes want absolutely nothing to do with you. I have been relegated to this status of social leprosy because of society's segregation of people like me. I've lost most of my friends because of my illness. When someone has heart disease or cancer, people shower them with "get well" cards and friendly, reassuring words. When you are told you are psychotic, you are treated very differently then people with other illnesses. This isn't because of the severity of the illness, but because most people just don't understand the disease so they don't know how to handle it. I feel very fortunate to have family and a few friends who are always there for me and will never judge me. My mom, dad, sister, Kieran, Anna, Snow White, and of course, my awesome cat, Vlad, have all been really supportive.

Still, my symptoms are usually very overwhelming. I often feel that everything in life is hopeless and that nothing I have done has ever mattered. Each decision I make feels like the wrong one. It's almost impossible to sleep and even harder to get out of bed every day and face the world. To have any sort of social interaction is terrifying for me. I have very little motivation and I'm always taking things the wrong way. I never want to go out and be with friends. When I do go out, I panic or I start hallucinating and have to leave. My energy level is shit. The things I used to care about are becoming less and less important to me. These are my every day symptoms and I think it's important for me to not keep them tied up inside.

As for my psychotic symptoms, I have some paranoid delusions and hallucinations. I often feel that I'm being followed or that some nameless person is planning to hurt my daughter and me. I hear people say things behind my back; when I look, there is no one there. But perhaps the most intense part of my illness is the communication I have with a woman from a parallel universe. Her name is Snow White (and yes, she dresses the part). When we first met, she told me that if I removed and devoured my own heart that I could join her in her universe where everyone lives forever. She showed me how to go about the task of removing and eating my heart. I have had many equally strange encounters with her. To me, she is just as real a person as anyone else and our conversations are as real as any dialogue could be. She is the one person that keeps me hoping that there is a better future in store for me. Even the subconscious and "psychotic" occurrences in our world are to Snow White more tangible than anything.

As I mentioned earlier, I have dissociative amnesia. This means that sometimes I completely lose time, much like one does during a blackout. This is also called a "fugue state." I'll be in one place and suddenly feel dizzy and realize I'm in another place and time has passed that I can't account for and I can't remember anything. I don't know how long they last exactly, but sometimes they seem to last for hours. I can no longer drive a car or ride a bicycle because of the blackouts. The blackouts usually happen when I'm in a stressful situation.

Last month I had a blackout and when I came to, my friend told me I had gotten into a fistfight. I went to the emergency room with a concussion. I then spent a few days in the psych ward. When I was released, I was told to stay in bed for three weeks because I couldn't risk falling down and hitting my head a second time. This meant that I had to cancel a show that RAW NERVES was scheduled to play. I've had to cancel before, but not very often.

I always thought that my band mates would be supportive and understanding. Nevertheless, the band felt that my disability had become too much of an inconvenience and they kicked me out. They didn't even have the guts to tell me face to face. I had to hear it over the phone. We had eight new songs that we were going to record the following month, a new record coming out in Europe, a West Coast tour planned for the spring, and split 7" with our good friends Acts of Sedition. Now, all of the hard work I had put into RAW NERVES over the past three years had been pulled out from under me. They quickly replaced me with a new singer and they did the tour without me. I have never felt so betrayed by people who I thought were friends.

I feel it is imperative that we wear our motives on our sleeves. The people involved in the spectacle of punk need to question why they are here, what they want to get out of punk, and how they are going to treat others in the process. I know it's easy to talk about what we dislike about our counter culture but we really need to focus on what we can do to make it better for everyone involved. We should be critical, but also ambitious to fix things. I have always felt it's important to call people on their shit when they do something that is fucked up. With the amount of social climbing that goes on in the punk scene in the U.S., it's important to get things like the treatment of punks with mental illness out in the open. The scene is becoming more and more like a high school social clique every day and the people who make it that way should be ashamed. The drama they create should be exposed so people can see it for what it is.

To make matters worse, the other band I was in, SQUALORA, broke up a few months after I was kicked out of RAW NERVES. Now, playing music, which was so therapeutic for me and which had kept me solid for so long, had completely collapsed. I've had to look for new ways to deal with my illness. I am trying making the best of it. I am back in school and studying for a degree in physics. School is very good because it keeps me occupied and keeps me from dwelling on all the bad things. But it doesn't fill the void that music has all these years, so I have kept writing songs and recording them as a solo project called BLEEDING TONGUES. I don't play shows or anything; I just record and release albums as a last ditch effort to keep myself from falling apart.

As disabled punks, we have to remember that we are a culture within a culture. We should always remember that punks are just like any other group of people. Some are self-serving, douche-bags while others are genuinely nice people. It's a constant process of weeding out the bad ones from the good ones. And at this point I can't trust anyone, including other punks.

People with disabilities are still people. We have to work twice as hard as anyone else. We deserve respect just like anyone else. We need to stay strong and not be ashamed of our illnesses. More than anything, we have to stick together and support each other when times are tough. No matter how bad things get, we must remember that it could always be worse. We must remember that, at least for this moment, we have our lives, however difficult they may be.

Contact: mattsvendsen@gmail.com

Pat's Story

Pat Thielges

There is a tree in my backyard that has a huge, far reaching branch on it, perfect for supporting a swing . Two years ago, I pretty much decided to go ahead and hang myself from that branch. I had it all planned out. I would use an extension cord to do it while I stood on a stepladder which was high enough to ensure that I would break my neck from the fall. I did my research. I would also make sure to close the curtains to the back yard and leave a note in the living room, telling either my wife or daughter to not go to the back yard, but to call the coroner and that I am sorry.

I have a wonderful wife, a teenage daughter, two dogs, a lot of friends, and workmates who would consider me a very funny person. I always wished that I could feel that way about myself, but I never could. I have clinical depression and I take a thirty milligram dose of Citalopram every day to make sure I don't feel like that ever again. I am glad I chose this route, as it took a lot of letting go on my end to finally come to terms with the fact that I wasn't just moody . . . I was sick.

I have been involved in the hardcore punk scene since 1983. I tend to enjoy my music on the angry side. I used to be a very angry kid.

I didn't come from a very warm and fuzzy home, I wasn't gifted at school, and I never was much good at meeting girls, so the scene was perfect for me and I was perfect for it. I always felt like I had a real hard time relating to my surroundings. I had a difficult time at jobs and at school because I felt confused a lot. I was uneasy about myself and I figured it is perfectly normal. I liked drinking . . . a lot! It set me apart from my friends because I was the guy that would get so fucked up it was almost dangerous. Drugs? Sure, why not? I felt normal only if I was either fucked up or coming down from being fucked up. When I wasn't totally ripped, my mind would go into overdrive like the way you talk when you are on coke, but it was in my head. I felt like I was the Tasmanian Devil from the *Looney Tunes* in there, and the things I thought when I was straight were not very pleasing. So, I would turn all that off. Easy . . . until it stopped working and the cure began to be worse than the symptoms. I lost a lot of friends, my first wife, money, and all that. I finally tried to get help at the . . . get this . . . Fayette County department of mental retardation and drug abuse . . . or something like that. It was a horrible government funded office. I had blood taken, went and talked to a Cuban shrink who told me to "take up a sport, go swimming, ride a bike" every fucking time I went to see him. He didn't give a shit. They put me on my first medication back then it didn't work. I felt like shit from the medicine and gave up on it. This was around 1998. I lived my life with this terrible problem for over a decade until I found myself looking at that fucking tree in my yard.

I am glad I took the step. I am glad I cannot be ashamed of my depression. I am not weak, or a crybaby. I have a medical condition and this medicine works for me. Sometimes I am afraid to think about what it would be like if my medicine stopped working. Sometimes I am afraid the medicine will make me do things I don't want to do. A lot of people feel that psych meds are a joke and that you don't need them. In some cases that may be true, but my life is changed for the better and I love every day. And someday I am gonna fucking cut that tree down in my yard and plant a new one.

More Than Just a Tag

Q

Dear You,

How powerful is a word?

I've often wondered what words mean in general. I can sit alone for hours saying and writing things over and over until they become merely sounds and/or shapes. I repeat them until, on some level, they all are meaningless.

Words can have a profound effect. They can be wielded for nice, fun, and even on some levels fulfilling reasons. Still, some words can be hurtful, painful, and downright depressing.

I think before I go any further with discussion, we should know one another a little bit better (or you should know me . . . or at least the "me" that I am willing to show you here in this letter). For the record, I have never been much of a writer and I have a tough time staying on point . . . so, please, bear with me.

I grew up in a lower-class family. I was shifted around every six months, or at least once a year, due to whichever parent I was living with at the time changing occupations or being sent to live with one parent by my other parent. This constant moving pattern lasted until

I was about ten. I didn't really get to know many people during this time. The people I did get to know, I didn't know for long. This is perhaps what helped cement some of my hermetic behaviors and antisocial feelings.

After I turned ten, things began to settle down and my wheels really took traction. I began to study things that I really wanted to learn about, such as math and chess. Math was always a great outlet for me and chess just seemed to lend itself to me with its subtle subplots. By the time I was twelve, I was a ranked chess player and I had received a few awards for being gifted in mathematics. I was really doing well and there wasn't a cloud in sight. By thirteen, I was looking at what colleges I wanted to attend and what I might want to do with my life. I was so interested in the future.

During this time, I also finally developed a few friendships—the kind I thought were going to last a lifetime. I met my two best friends in the Webelos. We pushed each other so hard to be the best at whatever it was that we were interested in and there was nothing we felt we couldn't do. I remember walking the Arrow of Light with them and becoming Boy Scouts together. I was so elated. Even as I write this, I smile thinking of those times. Life was magical and every door I came across was wide open. Unfortunately, this reality was something that was quickly coming to an end.

One night, I remember talking to my dad about some things I had seen and some ideas that I had had. After the conversation, I quietly proceeded into my room and listened to a record that I had just bought with my paper route money. I didn't think that much about the conversation I had just had with my father. However, my dad did think a lot about the conversation we had just had. The next morning, I went about my normal routine: I got up, made my bed, and ate my breakfast. Then something very different happened. Instead of walking to school, which was what I usually did, my father said that he was going to give me a ride. I noticed that one of my suitcases was in the car and we left the house heading in the wrong direction, but I didn't really care since school was kind of boring anyways.

When my dad and I did eventually stop, we were outside a pretty strange looking building that looked something like what might happen if you jammed a prison into a hotel. We parked the car and walked into the front office. Two strange men promptly whisked me away from my father, who refused to look at me. For some reason, my dad took it really well that I was being dragged away by two strange men who didn't seem keen on my resistance or my choice in language at the time.

Finally, I found out where I was: I was in drug rehab. What a crock?! I had never even done drugs and I was, in fact, dead set against them. I sat through hours of useless questions about my friends, about drugs, and about "we know what you're going through." The whole charade just went on and on. Eventually, they told me to pee in a cup and they took a vial of my blood. They then stuck me in a reception-like area that had a lot of wiry looking kids that seemed to be pretty nervous and upset about their current set of circumstances. I was only at the drug rehab for a couple days. Ultimately, my father, much to his chagrin, returned for me. I was so pissed at him; I really couldn't believe he had done this to me. We talked about the fact that I wasn't on drugs and that my drug test results came up negative, but we weren't even heading home. We were off to an office in a building full of people shuffling around aimlessly.

I waited a little while in a reception room with some lame *Highlights* magazines. Then I was stuck in a room with a man who "wanted to understand." He wanted to know what I thought of this issue or what I thought of that issue. I felt a little guarded because his line of questioning was similar to what I had just heard at the drug rehab for the past few days, but there was something just a touch different this time. I still had no idea why I was at this office (or had been in drug rehab), but I had a bad feeling that things were going to get a lot worse for me if I told this guy anything that he deemed unsettling. I tried to be banal and gave run of the mill answers. I figured that if I could beat my dad in chess, I could beat this guy and his questions.

After the guy was done talking to me, I sat out in the waiting room while my dad talked to the guy behind closed doors about whatever it was that they were so secretive about. As I sat there waiting, I figured that things were somehow still going to get worse for me. So, I did what I think almost anyone would have done: I got up walked out the door. I got in the elevator and ran away. I didn't make it that far since I really didn't have anywhere to go; I just went to my friend's house. Later that night, at my friend's house, my dad caught up with me. Upstairs, I could hear the adults going on and on about whatever it was that my dad was so worried about. I contemplated what I should do. My friends asked me what was going on and I didn't have an answer for them. This night was the last time I ever hung with either of them.

I spent about the next year of my life in a hospital. Everything in my life has turned out so different than I thought it was going to when I was younger. When I got out of the hospital, things were very different. My friends didn't really want to have anything to do with me and most people acted like I was a bad person. I got called a lot of names. The names, that I prefer not to get into, were really, really hurtful. I was treated like an outcast, a pariah. I was suddenly someone who was incapable of doing great things; I had been dismissed summarily. All those doors that were once wide open had been slammed shut. I felt pretty alone and turned to drugs . . . and man I turned to a lot of them.

After a few attempts at finishing high school, I eventually dropped out. I couldn't handle all the nonsense and the ceaseless beatings that I regularly received from several of my classmates. I had become something to beat on and disgrace for personal amusement. It sucked.

My dad didn't know what to do with me, so he shipped me off to be with my mother. I hadn't seen my mom since I was eight years old. I really didn't know her very well and I really didn't get to know her. She had a boyfriend who was an abusive alcoholic with a pension for violence—great guy. Life went on like this for a while with him beating the shit out of her, and at first she just started to turning first to Irish coffees and it really wasn't long after that she eventually just started popping pills, at the time a part of me thought that was pretty normal. Eventually I got in some trouble for giving my mom's boyfriend some of the same sensitivity he had enjoyed doling out so often. I never saw my mom after that event; it's something that has always plagued my thoughts.

I spent some time in a dysfunctional youth "rehab," which really didn't make things any better staring at a room made of concrete and metal since it would seem that when you think you're doing the "right thing." Certain people would tend to disagree. It wasn't long until even in that environment I was doped up and singled out . . . I pretty much gave up. I figured if this is life . . . fuck it.

For the next fifteen years, I spent a lot of time blaming the world for my problems. I got involved in sick relationships and even sicker friendships. It's really not worth getting into most of these stories since, for the most part; it was just me getting wasted and wondering why I made all these bad choices. It wasn't all bad. I can say, without a doubt if it wasn't for some of the people I met during this time, the people who accepted me, I don't think I'd still be here to write any of this down.

Here I am, though, all this time later. I have somehow put myself through school; I have somehow started a career; and I have somehow carved out a little something I can call stability. Still, I have a hard time sometimes and it's an almost daily struggle to stay focused on the things in life that I am working towards. What I have going for me is that I am stronger now and I feel that I have found purpose again. I'm still an avid chess player and I still love math.

It's been five years since my last psychotic episode. It is a moment in time that I can't even recall and one of many moments that has seemingly defined almost my entire adolescent and adult life. I've accepted I'm not like most people. The one thing, if anything, which I have learned over and over again, is that I am not this nonsensical tag that people may place upon me. I am me and that's pretty cool.

I'm not sure I have a point here or if this made any sense to you, the reader. I can say with certainty that I am glad you exist. No matter what you may think of yourself right now, on a very real and somewhat uncomfortable level, I am glad we had this chance to know one another.

Don't be afraid to be vulnerable—it is the way we all begin and it is the only thing that truly makes us all human.

Sincerely,

Q

124 over 12

In the time since I wrote the piece you have just read and completing the editing process a few things have happened that could be seen as germane, in light of our subject matter.

Perhaps, I was romantic in my view of how far I've come or something along those lines and in some ways I think writing the piece you have just read lead to a lot of the realizations and events that have unfolded since.

A few weeks ago I attempted to opt out of the living process, and if it wasn't for the efforts of a complete stranger, I would be dead. And, to be honest, I'm not convinced that I'm happy about this current set of circumstances, the scenario where I'm here alive trying to figure this shit out.

I have been thinking a lot about my mother, about my life, and about my career. I hardly know where to begin and thinking about a lot of this has proved to be a monumental struggle. I have a hard time letting people in and I guess I always have. I push people away and I use aggressive language and behavior to mask my inner sense of vulnerability.

I have recently had dinner with mom who I hadn't seen in twenty-four almost twenty-five years, it was interesting to meet her since it's almost like I didn't know her at all. I had been struggling with a manufactured memory of who she was as a person now, in lieu, of taking the time to actually get to know her. I have been so fearful for so long, that I'm not sure what or who I am anymore.

This process has made me think more about things that I have been apparently running from for the better part of my life. It hurts to let go of the things I have hidden behind all this time, it hurts to be myself since, in some ways, I'm not sure who I am anymore.

I have been having a whole bunch of conversations with others and with myself as of late trying to figure out what I really want with my life. For the longest time, I have been so absorbed in my work that I seemingly have forgotten what it is to be a person; well the person I am. I had dug in so deep that I was feeling numb to everything, and perhaps that's what I wanted and perhaps in some regards it was a necessary part of whatever process it is that I currently find myself in.

I feel really alone these days. One of the things I have been putting off accepting is that I have loved very few people and those I have loved I have pushed away as though they were trying to hurt me; which has only lead me to feeling like a failure and non-deserving of love. One of my friends hung himself about two months ago and

I found his body since it was in the room we had just been drinking coffee in, we had been talking about the struggle we both were having he was my only real friend. I went to work and acted as if nothing had happened since it hurt too fucking much too even allow my thoughts for this person to wander into my headspace.

I'm really scared to let the world back in to my fragile existence, I am almost petrified.

The last ten years, I have spent my time working in system dynamics mostly in manufacturing and trying to help rid every business of its problems and finding the underlying root issues, and I find a certain irony in that being the thing I have ended up being interested in, and I'm quite good at finding the problems; but it seems I am far better in some regards at burying my own.

I feel incredibly selfish right now, I feel out of balance, and, to be honest, I don't feel all that optimistic. I can't drive to work the same way anymore since I am constantly afraid that I might just finish what I started and then who knows . . .

I am really struggling with being proactive about my mental health right now or, at least, that's what I have convinced the conscious side of myself of, but it's hard.

So, here I am, standing at the proverbial crossroads. My work schedule slowly creeping back to its normal insanity, my personal life nonexistent, and, lately, I have been questioning even the things I thought might be helping me. I know I have more than two choices but at times it seems like there are just two.

I can walk into the darkness and just let the world finish me off or I can run into the darkness and give it everything I have in hopes of something better. I'm not sure what I'll do, but I have to do something.

I need to think about it and when I say "it," I mean me.

Demand More

Rachel

Walking down the street, I lose my energy. The yawns don't stop. The want to curl up in a ball and sleep. For who knows how long. The staring off into space. The feeling of myself wasting away. The constant gnawing at my body to give up.

The most accurate statement of depression I have heard recently is "depression hurts." Simple, but accurate. Sometimes, I believe that depression is simply my body chemicals. My body is not receiving enough endorphins (my body's way of saying, "Rachel, go work out"). That's how I've even come to justify my taking a pill every night: "Rachel, your chemicals just aren't right . . . now swallow." But other times, I think it's situational. For instance, when I'm having a great time with great people, depression stays away (eighty percent of the time). In many ways, I have given up trying to understand it. All I know is that right now, I need the medication. Without it, I'm a wreck. Sometimes I look at myself and see myself as weak because of this, but for right now, I know it's what I need.

Whether or not depression is situational or chemical, I never feel as if I master it. Each time I feel down, the experience is somewhat "new." I feel like each time I try to have a resolution to my problem, it's a different outcome. The horrible feeling is somewhat always the same, but there is no fixed way to resolve it. No fixed way to get it out of my body and mind.

When I am finally out from under the dark clouds of depression, I am soaking in the light of happiness for as long as I can. I am free— liberated, if you will. I am back to my normal self. (Although if I were to go all meta on myself right now, what is my normal?) I am me—the me that does not plunge into a pool of my own self-pity. I am back to being motivated, to organizing events on campus, to going to shows, to getting out of my room.

I go back and forth between blaming the individual and blaming the community for the inaction to solve the equation of depression. It's both. It's absolutely both, but sometimes I like looking for the black and white of situations (after all, our society does love those binaries). I try so hard to just find out whom to put the pressure on, yet I remain speechless.

There is nothing more I want to say about it. It drains me of the little amount of energy I have left in this winter. When summer comes though, where will my excuse go?

And here's where the punk community comes in—I demand more. I demand more dialogue, more nights to relax with friends, more support. I want to feel involved in a community that cares about whether or not I feel like jumping. I want a community that actually gives a shit instead of just acting like they give a shit—because let's face it, every year punk gets closer and closer to just being another subculture without culture. As much as shows help, there's more that I want from it. There's a family. Family means no one gets left behind, but sometimes I do feel left behind in the shadows. Please help me chug on.

I look back over this piece I wrote about a year ago and I pause to give a brief smile. Everything I've said here is true. Yet in the meantime, I've found out how extreme my physical dependence on my medication is. I slowly got off my sixty milligrams of Cymbalta: tapered to forty, then twenty, then pause for five months because I couldn't handle the rapid transition, then zero milligrams. Then, slowly I began to incorporate crying into my daily routine. Then, in a sudden whirlwind of two weeks, I was incorporating crying and yanking out my eyebrows into my hourly routine. Then, "Hello, I'm calling to schedule an appointment."

Recently, I have felt supported by the punk scene, and my family, in the process of getting back on the meds. Many loved ones in my life are not as fortunate (and there are others who refuse to seek the help they so desperately need). Please, watch those around you—please, be the best bystander you can be. See something, say something.

I'M CRAZY?

Sock

It seems like there are many situations and activities I choose to not participate in for my wellbeing. A lot of these things are really popular and mass-accepted as simply "what you do." To name a few: working towards and wanting a career, eating animals, mindless marriage and unhealthy monogamy/codependency, owning a car, drinking, drugging, going to bars . . . I feel like, in a sense, I have chosen to drop out, kind of like school repeated, where there is a form I'm expected to follow and pay my dues so I can eventually reach a respectable (boast-able) income, hoard of possessions and spouse and children and car(s) to earn respect from my peers, family, random people I interact with. I feel a pressure to compile some hard-working time, toiling for some company, (no matter which one so long as I'm working and making money,) take some vacations to really enjoy my life once a year or so and then retire, being able to proudly tell about spending "thirty years at the company." With health gone from years of dissatisfaction, stress, lack of time or energy to make quality food, develop quality relationships, be involved in meaningful activities, I can now be "secure" and not worry about money, no matter that there is not much joy in my life, if any. And was there ever?

This is not the case for everyone, but it is for so many. I know this from experience within my own family, from the messages in our local newspaper, mainstream corporate news, the standards conveyed in mainstream films and music, friends, and others I've talked to who relay a lot of the same stories, again and again. I recognize this pressure on me and happily reject obedience to it. This feels like a healthy and not a stubborn reaction, but resistance to norms comes naturally from knowing what is better for me. The rift I feel currently in my life is the tear between choosing not to disclose openly and honestly about my life, which includes unpopular, misunderstood, and possibly disgusting or hated parts to someone living a "normal" mainstream life. The energy it often takes to explain my perspective to more mainstream types wears on me and many times I choose to not disclose my thoughts and ideas. Sometimes, I'll feel on fire about expressing my views and I have the juice for it and not in a bragging "look at me" way but in a simple way of not wanting to feel shame or need to hide aspects of who I am. The accumulation of little bits of uncertainty to share myself builds up and forms stress, painful blockages born of unproud living.

I'm interested in the free feelings of expressing myself proudly with no need for approval and no care if there's criticism. That sureness and open-mindedness feels the best. This sureness of myself and my needs doesn't equate to sharing my opinions every single time—I don't always need to put in my piece, and often I feel great resisting the urge to share my opinion. It feels shitty when I find myself expressing myself in a way that has egoic motivations behind it like the desire to stand out, be praised, noticed, and/or validated. The self-validation, I feel, from security in who I am, trumps any outside approval. While sometimes I may choose to share my opinions, other times it feels great to keep quiet, and I do my best to be real with myself about the energy expelled in certain situations and with particular people.

I don't want to fight to convince someone my opinion matters so much. If they're closed off to a respectful conversation and are in a competitive mode, stepping aside and knowing that the energy I would have to expend would not be worth it feels really good.

They can "win" and I'll "win," within myself, by not creating more stress that comes with trying to defend this idea of myself.

Sometimes, when confronted directly, I change the subject or avoid it. I try not to outright lie, but sometimes it seems better for the person I'm talking with. I don't like this, and I'm not totally okay with it, but as of now in my life, sometimes this is what I do. A part of me, for sure, yearns to disclose the real, hard-to-spit-out truth. I know it will feel good once we get past the discomfort, as everything always is in my experience, and is better than the nauseating, gut-wrenching feeling I get when I don't say what's really going on.

Other times, I just feel like what they don't know won't hurt them. I feel torn with my choice to not tell my parents that I have a vasectomy, assuming it will bum them out to know that they will never have a grandchild from me. My thinking is that I will cause them great pain by disclosing this information, and there is definitely fear of confrontation and their disapproval there, and I wonder and debate with myself whether telling them could create intimacy and trust between us or just cause them hurt. It would feel amazing if they respected and understood my decision to not have children, but that doesn't feel necessary. I can see their disapproval being worth the honesty created between us, and ultimately that's what I want in my life—honesty, with others' approval or not. I am tired of hiding my life, I want to be proud of what I do and live in that way.

Subconscious guilt, shame, and self-hatred cumulate in a way that rots us from inside and I don't want to put myself thru this. The debate is raised when you're dealing with a straight world that requires huge amounts of energy to explain your radical ways, your mental struggles, and many things that are foreign concepts. It feels too much, a lot of the time, and you can be met with looks of disgust, for example, when you back out of going to a social gathering because you feel nervous about it. I have done this and have gotten looks of confusion from my friends or family and they say things wondering why I don't want to go or why I can't just pull myself together, it will be fun. This sounds terrible and explaining to them how I want to go but feel terrified is scary to do because it's an insecure part of myself that I don't fully understand and it takes a lot of bravery and energy that I don't always have to explain that to them. And sometimes when I do have the energy, it doesn't make sense to some people, which is okay, but it becomes not okay when they don't have any empathy to the anxiety I may be feeling and I go through the trouble to explain to a person who looks annoyed and is absent of compassion. It's easy for me to then slip into feelings of alienation, sadness, and protection of this persons demeanor onto the whole world. I, quickly, can find myself thinking thoughts about how the is cold, cruel and, for sure, the world I am experiencing has that feel to it. It is empowering to be true to yourself in the face of adversity, and I'm so interested in finding low energy expending ways to live this.

Especially with the vasectomy situation, I know my reasons and don't need support. I struggle with the idea of bringing a life into this world, a seemingly decaying and sick one, with of course beauty and value that exists as long as you are able/willing to seek it out. The potential genetic inheritance of debilitating mental patterns of mine is also pretty unnerving to think of passing onto my child that has no say in the matter of even existing and navigating their life with things like heavy dread that comes out of nowhere and feelings of exhaustion with the world and wanting to stop living. I'm confident in my decision to have gotten a vasectomy and I don't need any one else's approval, but I do experience feelings of hurt for not getting validation from my parents. Ultimately, many of my decisions and beliefs will never be good with them, and it would rule for them to accept those parts of me, but that might be too much to ask. It comes down to the life I want to live, and it being at odds with theirs, and that's all there is to it. Hopefully we can agree to disagree, and not in some passive aggressive, bitter way, but in an unconditional loving way. You don't need to understand and agree with someone to love them.

So, I think dropping out of a lot of normal mainstream modes of living can tie in directly to a thriving mental state. Sometimes, the world is too much to deal with, and alternative forms of entertainment, therapy, eating to what is the norm are necessary to not feel like you are in a completely hostile place. I need to seek out and create these alternatives to standard practices that I can't participate in very regularly if I don't want to feel disgust and disdain that spirals into despair and hopelessness. Of course, a lot of things are unavoidable and some days I find myself able to laugh it off and continue with what needs to get done. There are other days I am debilitated and unable to carry out responsibilities that remind me of the unbalanced, greed-driven capitalist system that we live in. Living within a patriarchal society, one that seems to be led by a mantra of "more, no matter at what cost" that produces things that create filth and never decompose, that prioritizes white males, and is a world led by a few rich, white males, that fucks up non-human animals through the food system, entertainment, and "medical" research/experimentation, and human animals abusing and hurting others, trying to feel some power in their own lives, it all feels so overwhelming and unstoppable.

"Ignorance is bliss" is something I've heard as a possible solution. "Don't think about it so much." But I don't feel willing or even able to gouge out my eyes, so to speak, in order to find an ignorant peace with what's going on. The feelings of apathy, of stagnation, and inaction are the most destructive, brain-rotting, empty feelings I know. Sometimes a treat or vacation of sorts from the work you do is needed, but a permanent, "Fuck it, I'm just going to enjoy myself" thing leaves a gaping hole for me and brings more stress and depression than enjoyment. I experiment with different forms and quantities of escapism, and I need them, but the frequency and content of them makes or breaks it. An escape for me, for example, tonight was the thought of going bowling. Rolling a ball down a lane to knock over pins is pretty fun for me, having fun with friends or alone. For a little bit.

Spending the money to be entertained is not, however. And there are some hard-to-describe feelings of lack I feel upon leaving the bowling alley. Not a despair, super heavy feeling, like when I think about the popularity of woman-hating rappers like Eminem, but a mild, mild discontent, a knowing that there are so many other fucking things I'm wild about! It's the feeling of settling. I don't want to make a big deal about it, like I'm against bowling. Bowling's fun! I like it! But when do you fucking go for it, tackle the shit you love, that isn't so easy to get started, unlike the bowling game that you ride your bike over to, pay five dollars, and it's all set up for you? And moderation is key—I couldn't be in a bowling league but I can go a few times a year and have fun.

Bowling, movies, and going out to eat are all distant the fulfillments of creating! Creating isn't always so easy! So I find myself delaying the challenging stuff, because it's not so easy to get into, it's not so thrilling when you don't feel inspired. Living within a world where maybe you only see cars and billboards and mainstream lies, news all around you, you can't find the gumption to pick up that paintbrush or pencil or spatula that you know is so vital to the life you want to live. It has saved you before, and it will again, but you don't remember because you are being sucked into the grey void of the culture-less; follow the path, work, sleep, retire, die in mass-accepted, mass-practiced conformity. Knowing this, and getting sucked in makes me feel deflated because I didn't create and blaze my own path. Instead, I turned on the computer and all of a sudden I've spent the last hour looking at videos on the internet that lead one in to the other, mildly entertaining and containing no worth to remain in my head and bring any kind of satisfaction. You can get your pleasure fix for a minute, maybe have a laugh, tell some people, maybe email a link, and you settled.

Ignoring the rhythms of my heart and taking the boring, mass-accepted, easy path accumulates in my psyche when I take that route too often or too intensely.

I think a lot about how to foster creativity and inspiration. Over the years I've been looking at my individualist mindset that keeps me from reaching out, often under the idea that I don't want to be a burden to others. I'm realizing and experiencing the interconnectedness of people and how asking for help can be such a help to others, letting them know that you trust them and value their abilities to help you out. I've contemplated mental health in a community sense, instead of a hyper-individualist way and dreamed of creating encouraging, safe, passionate environments that can help ground and stabilize us. I envision them as inspiring places helping me blast off into hyper, productive, explosions of creativity or comfortable relaxing places to get support and feel okay about feeling bad.

Positive communities of like-minded folks can encourage these creative adventures, literally through words, or maybe just by being in a place that nurtures care and love and makes someone feel their best and thus inspires creative expression and true living of life. These followings of the passions that make our hearts burst, is top priority to me. I, and many others would do good to construct healthy habits and live out these passions.

Sometimes, dropping out from the "normal world" is scary, and socially unacceptable, but ultimately necessary. Maybe dropping out in certain moments, periodically, as one learns that that is what they need, or maybe when it all seems too much and you feel like you're going to start crying . . . or slitting throats. It's interesting, those challenging courses of action that are ultimately immeasurable in their reward to you, but can be so tricky to get going at! Often, I feel like the mainstream route is one of laid out paths that are easy to slide into, but unearthing our passions and letting them lead us, though it may take more work, pays off.

My younger sister and I had a recent conversation about writing, and she asked me if I felt the compulsion to write. "Yes, definitely," I said. I went on to say it seemed too hard sometimes, though. She then sent me an awesome essay entitled "Shitty First Drafts" which went on to say almost no one gets it right the first time, and through perseverance, quality writing can come about. This was encouraging, because I always have felt insanely intimidated by revision and editing, and, usually, just go with the first draft, feeling impatient and untrusting of the process that could bring about a better finished piece. I have started to attempt these revision processes and enjoy them (as I am doing right now) and it feels in line with other themes of my life where patience is needed. My manic highs often come after depressive despair type feelings, and I find myself rushing to utilize my creative spark and document my epiphanies. There is great joy in these explosions but, definitely, a nervous edge. Difficult as it is to retrain myself, it is definitely doable. It takes a good amount of discipline which I am working on implementing more in my life to bring about the satisfaction that comes with self-trust. You can re-find your creativity and working at it instead of waiting for the post-depression sunshine spark. It's empowering to try to foster this inspiration instead of hating the world and falling into funks; dreaming that I was a different way than I am.

Working past my fears of the manic moments waning, and that what I have to write or rewrite in the revision process will lack passion, I write now to remember that it is worth the effort. I would like to say I'm not lazy about it, but I feel that often, as real as my dark moments are, I almost want to stay trapped in pain. I want to feel bad for myself. Maybe because it's familiar? The moments of no inspiration feel scary, I begin to overthink that I am becoming or am already boring and I have lost to the drab, grey world I hate. I can't help but wonder and want to continue to experiment with the skewed perception I have with doing. Reframing my mindset and the attempts at garnering inspiration as "doing" rather than "trying" can help to develop a healthy point of view that the trial, in itself, is something. When I tell people that I write they begin to talk of getting published. While there isn't something inherently wrong with getting published, that does not constitute success for me. Success is being there for the writing, enjoying the process, and not wanting to be somewhere else. Isn't that a successful moment, a successful life? It's the immersion in it, relishing that you are there, knowing that you are a part in the dance of life. What more can we want, what can we ever measure, and how can that drive for a sense of "making it" in whatever way, truly, drive us to frustration, routine dissatisfaction, or even madness?

My sister also told me about how she constantly reads quotes from other writers about how challenging, and often, mind-numbing the writing process can be! This surprised me because I have never considered myself a "real" writer because of my difficulty with the writing process and assumed that professional writers do not struggle and the words flow out endlessly and effortlessly. I wasn't and am not under the delusion that getting published makes you a writer but it was comforting for me to know that I'm not alone in the struggle for creation and inspiration and it's encouraging to persist and not give up on writing.

I love and work at maintaining a healthy balance between knowing my individual needs, methods, and desires and valuing having a part in a community. Feedback, encouragement, and the nurturing of love and care with each other is so vital to maintaining groups of people with strong bonds, focusing on what is important to them and finding like minds for support and reassurance in a straight world that may devalue and destroy what you love.

Feeling utter despair with the state of things, and feeling burnt out on humanity in general, it's easy to fall into depression. It can feel like it's pointless to do anything when shit seems very seriously unfixable and you seem to only notice humans being cruel to each other and all life. At the pace we are going, it seems like human life could end in my time, and at the least a pile of toxic garbage and dying earth will be left for the next generation. It makes me so fucking mad, and breaks my heart, and not doing something about it, slouching into apathy, is the unforgiveable, impossible path that I will never ever take. Resisting, raising a stink, knowing that those of us who value equality, justice, and life full of joy, love, and community, like it is meant to be, are not wrong! The fuckers who destroy the earth and cause so much pain are wrong! They are crazy!

Feeling sorrow at the state of things is not crazy! It is crazy to accept all of this as logical and not see the destruction and cruelty in violent capitalist systems! I know I, and many of us, need to keep resisting; keep building positive, productive, giving communities and we need to not be afraid to ask for help! The world needs more people to ask for help! Don't be afraid to cry, to say you feel depressed, anxious, fucked up. Find friends and romantic partners who help you be a better person, who help you thrive and encourage you. If your family is not supportive, find a new family of friends. You don't have to keep taking abuse just because you are related by blood to someone.

Life goes so quickly, and sometimes can seem like a cruel joke. My brain tends to spin out of control and I feel alone, useless, pathetic. This is not true, there is so much to live for, and resignation to be an accepting, unquestioning robot who is "secure" in every way except the securement of that giddy feeling of passion for being alive, is a waste of your life, my life, of all life. I think we would do good to ourselves if we kept reassuring ourselves that we are not crazy and not let an insane world convince us otherwise.

Throughout this resistance, this fiery reclamation of our lives I know it's crucial to be patient, to let ourselves take breaks, and to be supportive when it's all too much and we don't feel like warriors. It can be overwhelming. So many burn out and sell out and join the rat race because they had such lofty goals and dreams that they didn't see measurable results to. To many an extent, we are blind in our efforts and we have to do our best because that may be all we can measure. It's that rich knowing that we gave it our all, no matter the world's reflection back to us as losers. In such adversity and difficult odds, it's important to hold fast to this assurance that we did all one person could do and to be nice to ourselves and real about what we can do. Take a break from your life if you need, and come back to it. Get creative, get in touch with other folks, stay busy, take rests, don't accept the norm, do whatever your heart tells you! I'm not crazy! You're not crazy! We're not crazy!

Having to Do With

Synthia Nicole

Being diagnosed with anxiety and depression in my mid-twenties was a release, in a few ways. On the one hand, I could relax, but another way it can be taken is like a broadcast. It was now public with my mental health professionals. My psychologist mentioned that I had probably been dealing with these issues, at least, since my suicide attempt in seventh grade, which led me to the mental health unit. Looking back, I can remember how some episodes felt, but honestly it doesn't feel too good, knowing that nothing at the time made sense to me. Man, then I'm immediately feeling relieved for having "been there and somehow survived."

After a MMPI (Minnesota Multiphasic Personality Inventory), when I was diagnosed, I was offered medication for these issues. I questioned the suggestion, only for a moment. I asked about alternatives then decided to ride my bike harder and do yoga more often.

On June 11, 2004, I had a brain injury that lead to three brain surgeries and partial removal of my cerebellum. Other areas of my brain were affected, but they can't really tell how much of what. Or, maybe I don't recall. I also acquired a memory deficit. After about a month into my hospitalization in the rehabilitation unit, a woman was sent in to talk with me. I cried the whole time. The next morning, my doctor came in, as usual, saying that the woman I talked to suggested I be on an antidepressant. I declined. Then he said, "Well, Synthia, I think so too." I trusted his opinion enough because he visited me every day. I then agreed.

Soon after, I began to get "outside of myself," as in being able to focus on more and not feel so devastated for the things I would now never be able to carry out (I could barely walk, didn't have breath support, and was speaking monotone. Plus, I had a myriad of other problems.). I, somehow, decided to concentrate on the tasks in front of me.

After being at the county hospital for a few months, I was transferred to a center for people with disabilities for a few more months. Upon my release, I moved in with my parents. Following this, I thought it would be okay if I experimented with a lot of herbal supplements with my "new" self. I had set up a supplement for each of my "traditional" medications. My experiment was an experience. Looking back, I should have built up these herbal supplements for about a month in my body. Turns out, I cried at the drop of a hat for a whole month.

I had never thought much of antidepressants and antianxiety medication until after my injury and that experiment. My symptoms have become worse, yet addressed and somewhat manageable. I'm grateful to have a physician, psychiatrist, psychologist, and pain psychologist who are on my side (well, three out of four isn't bad) and who are able to contact each other. They also know I'm a recovering alcoholic. Yep, I have had a nineteen-year using career, consisting of drugs and alcohol. That has had quite an effect on my depression and anxiety. I carried my life out with a "fuk shit up" attitude. I am becoming more honest about my situation(s), especially with myself and asking for help and acceptance.

I found The Icarus Project (http://theicarusproject.net/) in 2008. It's a radical mental health community that has online discussions and forums. Actual meetings take place in some cities. Their subtitle is, "Navigating the space between brilliance and madness." Worth a look-see!

Synthia Nicole writes the zine *Damaged Mentality*.

More Synthia Nicole available at:
http://wemakezines.ning.com/profile/chinagirl
http://www.mnartists.org/artistHome.do?rid=343400
Boneshaker Books in Minneapolis & Quimby's Bookstore in Chicago

Damaged Mentality zine is on Facebook—I'm there.

For further support, *Filling the Void* zine is available at dorisdorisdoris.com

Second Chance at a First Class Life

Talon Demeo

Boredom equaled danger. Temptation was its best friend. It was scary just how easily I'd forget the pain I'd been in from a night or week ago. It was like I had a built in forgetter. I knew I had a problem. You'd think I would have learned by then that knowledge was not wisdom. My innocence was ripped away from me. I felt overwhelming disarray. My optimistic point of view completely abandoned me and I was living just to get drunk or well from the sickness of my narcotic addiction. I was searching for the answer to remedy my soul.

For years, I looked outside myself to fill this empty hole, when all along the answer was inside my heart. I walked the streets full of pain. I broke into cars and boosted goods to survive. I woke up dopesick, in many squats and crawled to the dope spot. Puking bile with a rotting stomach and a runny nose dripping snot. Incomprehensible demoralization made me homicidal. I'd smash a victim, take his wallet, and leave him for dead. Then, I'd barely make it to the dope spot because of how sick my body was. No one would be out because it was too hot. My "jones" would make me desperate and some fucking asshole would rip me off. This went on for years, until, I went to prison for assaulting someone while I was drunk. That's when I had had enough. I hit my bottom, so to speak. While incarcerated, I had a spiritual awakening. No, I didn't see God or find religion, I just realized that if I kept having insane thoughts, then my actions would keep producing bad consequences.

That's when I got into meditation and prayer. I figured if I meditated on good thoughts, then my actions will produce good consequences. And if I fuck up, I can just admit that I did wrong and learn from it and move on. Instead of being a victim, I can be a student.

Today my life is good. I have a daily program that involves exercise, eating right, meditation, and helping others so I can get out of my own fucked up head. It's like walking up the down escalator. I gotta keep on keeping on, or I'll get sucked back into the vortex of my insanity. Art and music also help a lot. It's very therapeutic for me, as it's a good outlet for my anger and trauma.

I'm not really sure why I'm still alive. If life was fair, I'd be dead ten times over. But I'm not. I guess the powers that be have other plans for me, and I think my new purpose in life is to be of service to others and spread some kind of message of recovery to the people who still suffer. May my life's energy benefit all beings.

The Nature of the Beast

Thomas Reitmayer

Sit back and let me tell you about the sadness
About the beast that's been gnashing its teeth, trying to destroy me (. . .)
It snarls at me
It hides underneath my bed
It sinks its teeth in every corner of my head.
(Off With Their Heads)

Five years ago, I got the diagnosis: emotionally unstable personality disorder. Hung over. In a hospital. It was a diagnosis delivered from a doctor who could not care less about me and who did not even explain whatever the fuck that meant. On one hand, it felt like a verdict: you, my friend, are now a lifer. Fucked forever. On the other hand, it was almost a revelation. I finally had a tag I could put on that beast under my bed and all the years of feeling like shit, were now summed up in four words. I believe some people must feel like this when they find god. Or the devil, for that matter.

I always knew that something was wrong with me. For lack of a better term, I felt "wrong." I felt out of step with the world. I was more sensitive than my peers, less resistant to stress, more caught up in my own world of books and records, more . . . wrong. Four-year-old boys usually don't spend nights awake, trying to hide their tears. Four-year-old boys usually want to be hugged by mom or dad and find solace. Four-year-old boys do not usually rub their four-year-old dicks until they are sore because there is no other way to deal with the panic attacks at night, the tension, and the fear. It's surprising how many strategies for coping a person can come up with just to survive: drink oneself to sleep, fuck complete strangers in order to forget one's loneliness for a night, break one's hand or nose in a fight so that one can, at least, feel something . . . the possibilities are endless.

> Don't try to stop it
> Don't try to control it
> Don't try to defeat it
> Don't try to console it
> It's unstoppable
> And it's a part of me.
> (Off With Their Heads)

I am thirty-eight years old now. My body is full of scars: scars from fights and self-inflicted scars or scars from the countless fights I picked. Oh, I was quite the fighter. I fought everything and everyone, including myself. It was fight, fuck, fail. I fucked myself with bottles, substances, and women. Ultimately, I fucked myself up, myself and others. It was all just because I could not deal with the pain and the emptiness. They say that the worst kind of loneliness is the loneliness that's shared with others. I have lived and breathed that loneliness— and I have survived it.

The mental health system (or, as a fellow punk once called it, "mental *hell*th") is, entirely, fucked up. I was in therapy for years and years on end. I was on all kinds of drugs—medical and, for lack of a better term, recreational. The only things I ended up with were a dry mouth, diarrhea, shaking hands, uncontrollable sweating, a skyrocketing libido or no libido at all, complete lack of appetite, and too much sleep or insomnia. Not once, during my years of therapy and medication therapy, was I "all right." It really is no surprise to me that the word "therapist" is very similar to "the rapist."

A simple equation: I have known about my disorder for five years now, which means I spent more than thirty years not knowing at all. My ignorance to illness was largely because no one really cared or understood. Once I was diagnosed, everyone expected me to get better in the blink of an eye and to function like the rest of them. What they weren't recognizing was that I had basically been robbed of my life. What therapy did to me was basically make me completely lose my grasp on my emotions. I have found out the hard way that dissecting every little micro-detail of one's life is not only a very bad idea, it is completely wrong. Hopelessness? Check. Despair? Check. Irrationality? Check. Like Fugazi said,

> Hey man, I know where you're coming from.
> Yeah? Bullshit!!!

The thing is this: these emotions (hopelessness, despair, and irrationality) are completely normal. Everyone feels them to some extent: some feel them less than others and some feel them more than others. What my therapists did was isolate these emotions and made the emotions exist in a vacuum. This just blew everything out of proportion and made me feel worse, more wrong, and sicker.

> You've got me all wrong
> It's not the real me screaming you away
> It's that selfish sadness ruining every day
> Everything is wrong.
> (Off With Their Heads)

So, what actually is emotionally unstable personality disorder? It is the monster under your bed. It is spending all the money that you don't have on booze to make sure you fall asleep. It is taking your medication early and being awake still at four AM because you're too scared to fall asleep. It is waking up at six AM and unable to get the fuck out of bed because you're too scared to make it through the day. It is washing your dishes and taking extra care of your knives. It is going to a party just so you're not alone and then hating the party. It is hating people. It is hating yourself. It is hating going home alone and it is hating going home with someone else. It is not taking a shower for a week. It is taking a shower and looking at your scars, wondering where the fuck they came from. It is looking at your scars. It is looking at your scars, asking yourself over and over and over again what happened. It is a deathwish because life seems too unbearable. It is a deathwish because you are too fucking afraid to live. It is writing suicide notes in your head late at night in bed, but never finishing them because you feel too worn down to get out of bed and write them down. It is wanting to die more than wanting to live. It is wanting to die, but being ashamed of it and never telling anybody. It is wanting to die and finally telling someone, just to be laughed at. It is walking up the street to the gas station late at night when the temperature is unbearable outside to buy two beers. It is buying two beers that you can't afford. It is buying two beers and starving the next day. It is starving and enjoying it. It is being angry at your lover and wanting to jerk off. It is angry sexual fantasies of violent fucking and not making love. It is wanting to fuck but being unable to get an erection. It is taking a double dose of your medication. It is being unable to fall asleep for hours. It is getting out of bed, putting on your favorite record, and hating it. It is listening to your favorite record for hours and not feeling shit. It is turning the volume way the fuck up and still not feeling anything. It is wanting to sell your entire record collection. It is fucking complete strangers so that someone is nice to you, even if it's just for a moment. It is forgetting about it the next minute. It is fucking yourself. It is fucking yourself up. It is fucking yourself with a boy, a girl, a knife, a bottle, a nightmare, a book, a poem, your hand, cigarettes. It is wanting to go to the hospital at three AM. It is refusing to go the hospital. It is eventually going to the hospital and laughing at yourself for being such a pussy. It is giving yourself prison tattoos. It is hiding your tattoos. It is proudly displaying your tattoos. It is "be here to love me." It is "stay the fuck away from me." It is what it is.

An emotionally unstable personality disorder is a parody of life and human nature itself. The disorder poses the eternal question and it positions a person between the yes and the no at the very same moment, constantly, forever. It all comes down to two things. These two things tear you the fuck apart: "I love you" and "I hate you." These two emotions are so diametrically opposite and so strong that the constant tear between them causes you to eventually decide not to feel anything at all anymore. The solution is to just numb the pain. And then, once you are have numbed yourself, you wish for an emotion. You even wish for pain—any feeling that would make you feel alive.

There are moments when life is all ok. You get to live in those moments. You feel alive. You feel loved. You feel saved. These moments are when the floodgates break. These moments are when all the pain comes rushing over you.

> This is the part I wouldn't show you
> The part where you say: I don't even know you.
> (Jawbreaker)

I have lived through it all and I have survived. Ultimately, what it all comes down to is one simple thing: acceptance. Once you have understood that it's not some kind of flu that can be cured by medication and sleep, it all gets easier. It will never disappear. It will never be just okay. It will never be all right. You have read the contract with the devil and you have signed it; it said: life sentence. You were born, abused, you grew up, and you die. That's basically all there is to it, nothing more, and nothing less. If you work hard enough, it will get bearable at some point. You can lead a life—not a normal life, but a life nonetheless. And if you are lucky enough, like me, you will find a partner who does not only accept it, but a partner who understands it and even loves it. Make no mistake; it is a part of you. When you realize this, this is where the switch gets flicked—this is when you learn that it is okay. The key to the healing process is to be brutally honest to yourself and to others. Tell yourself where you fucked up. Tell your partner when "it" strikes and seek comfort and shelter, no matter how scared you are. This is your cure. There is no other way. It either is pure love or it is pure hate. That's the nature of this beast. This is who you are, for better or worse.

Punk and Therapy, the alternative way

Willem Visser

F irst, I want to thank Craig of *Upheaval* zine for giving me the op-portunity to write about and address the topic of mental illness. I have never been diagnosed as mentally ill, myself, but I've had quite a lot of therapy and would like to share my experiences about it.

In the punk scene, there are a lot of people with psychological problems or have close relatives with these problems. It is probably the reason why many of us are attracted to punk in the first place.

It is the perfect outlet for our anger and depression. Musically, there are more interesting genres but the intensity of punk doesn't have an equal. Punk lyrics are often about personal issues like depres-sion, isolation, and suicide but it is taboo to speak openly about them. Within the punk scene and "normal" society, emotional issues and psychological problems often go unspoken.

What is mental illness exactly? Psychiatrists in the U.S. have pub-lished a book entitled *Diagnostic and Statistical Manual of Mental Disorders* (*DSM*), a guideline to diagnose mental disorders. Whether it is depression or schizophrenia, you have to meet different criteria to be diagnosed with a specific disorder. Some of the defined illnesses are quite clear. Others, especially depression and attention deficit hyperactivity disorder (ADHD), are less clear.

For example, to be diagnosed with ADHD you have to match nearly six-of-nine subjective points to be diagnosed. It is great, for some, when the problems they face can be categorized as a certain illness. On the other hand, there is also a lot of abuse of the system by physicians, who use the guidelines of *DSM*, to prescribe drugs. The pharmaceutical industry has a huge interest in how mental issues are defined.

Many of the researchers that worked on *DSM*-defined mental illnesses were, in some way, financial influenced by these companies. That is a real conflict of interest.

Sixty years ago, ADHD didn't exist. Since it was defined in *DSM* millions of kids have been diagnosed with it. I'm not trying to play down all of the issues that people with ADHD have but the real winners are the companies that produce Ritalin.

The biggest problem I have with the current medical establishment isn't just their corrupt entanglement with the pharmaceutical industry; it is also their attitude.

The most important goal of most psychiatrists is to make their patients "function in society." Luckily, as someone who was influenced by the alternative ideas of punk, I'm really skeptical about what it means to function "normally" in society. Isn't normality just suppression? Our society is so fucked up, emphasized by the millions of people who would not be able to function if they weren't drugged with Valium or Xanax. Do you call that normal? Prescribing someone drugs so you can have a pharmaceutical-sponsored weekend get-a-way? Is that curing someone? A good therapist or psychiatrist should find the root cause of the issues and heal their patient.

About five years ago, I went through a hectic time with a lot of ups and downs. I started my first serious relationship. It was great to meet the right person, to be really close with someone, and share all of my love and joy. I was really happy and in love but the sex and intimacy triggered something. I started to have sleepless nights with terrible nightmares. During the day I was wrecked and very emotional. Sitting on the train, listening to my mp3 player, I would suddenly feel tears running down my face. Every movie I watched would touch me much more than usual and make me cry, real EMO style!

The insomnia got worse and I was afraid to go back to sleep. During the day, I was fearful. If I was walking down a busy street or stuck in a crowded subway car, anxiety would take control over me. A couple of times I almost lost control and made a huge scene in public places. I felt like randomly hitting people, screaming, or just running away and collapsing into a little corner. Somehow, I managed to keep control. For a long time I was too stubborn to ask for help or talk about my issues with friends. It felt like there was no way out. I was at the verge of a breakdown. My girlfriend, who had been a huge support, suggested I go to a hypnotherapist.

Looking back, it seems like a really obvious thing to do but, at the time, it felt like a huge step. It was a great relief to just talk openly to someone about my feelings and fears. I talked about all of my strange frightening nightmares, my family, and my past. Hypnotherapy was different than I imagined. Most of the time I would just sit and talk. A really effective technique was to let me go to my feelings and pay attention to them. Or, he would literal put me in different chairs, one chair represented my fears, one for my inner child and one as an observer. I would get to know different parts of myself, parts that I had suppressed.

Slowly, memories from the past came up in the sessions and in dreams at night. Sometimes strong physical memories, voices in my head, or scenes from the past that looked like a black and white movie.

It only took a couple of sessions to find the root cause of all my issues; abuse and trauma from my early childhood. This was a huge shock for me. I always thought I had a perfectly happy childhood and it took a lot of time to accept that it hadn't been what I thought it was. On the other hand, it began to make sense and explained a lot of things to me. Most importantly, recognizing what had happened was really healing for my inner child.

As a child, you can't defend yourself and you cannot or are not allowed to express all your anger and grief. I developed my own defense mechanisms and suppressed my trauma. It caused my behavioral patterns and created tension in my body, like armor. As an adult, in therapy, I comforted to my inner child and worked to get rid of my patterns. It took a lot of time and effort and the hypnotherapy helped me a lot with this.

There was still a lot of anger I could not get rid of and my therapist could not get to it. He suggested a bioenergetics session. Bioenergetics is based on Reichian Therapy, which focuses on the release of trauma through physical exercises and letting go of your emotions. Wilhelm Reich is a really interesting man. He was a pupil of Sigmund Freud. Check him out on the internet!

The people who gave the session were from the Osho Community and half of the people taking part were also Osho people. At the start, I was a bit shocked by their intimacy. Osho members give each other long hugs all the time. They were cool though.

The weekly bio-energetic sessions were a huge relief for me. I continued with it for two years. After out of control dancing for half hour on rhythmical music, I would get more and more in touch with my body. More grounded. Movements and breathing exercises would build up to a huge catharsis. Everybody was kicking and punching on a mantra. I would completely lose my mind and scream my head off. No! No! Really deep anger and hatred were released and stress in my body would go. Afterwards I felt really grounded and almost a bit high. A lot of the movements in the bioenergetics exercises were familiar to me because they were like moshing!

There was punching with the elbow to the back, kicking with the legs, floor punching, and the chopping of imaginary wood! All the exercises had to be combined with heavy breathing or screaming. All the ingredients of a good punk show. In a way, letting go at a concert is like a bioenergetics session. Damn, I can't count how many times I felt down and shitty but after a punk show I felt like I was reborn, having enough strength to face things again.

Between the therapy sessions, I would have a lot of cathartic moments at punk shows and listening to records. I would punch my fists into the wall screaming along to Negative Approach and go berserk on Bad Brains. Is there a record that captures rage and hatred better than *My War* by Black Flag?

That same year I finished my first zine, *Jagged Visions #1*, which, in way, was a form of creative therapy. It was an outlet for the things that were going on in my head, which is visible when you read the zine. Doing the interview and article on noize legends, Whitehouse, was quite cathartic. In another way, the zine was a way of really showing and expressing myself, to step out of my corner.

It took a year, but I felt much stronger about myself. Sometimes there are still moments when I struggle with things but I don't feel so fragile, stressed and out of control. I don't think mainstream therapy would have helped me as much. Bioenergetics, sports, and yoga helped me to feel so much better.

I had so many positive experiences I became eager and curious. I started taking therapy courses. A lot of techniques my hypnotherapist used were Neuro-Linguistic Programming (NLP) techniques. I was intrigued by their effectiveness and logic. I decided to become an NLP practitioner. It was really great and I learned a lot about myself. I also took several Reiki courses, a Japanese therapy that uses hand placement to transfer energy.

Right now, I'm finishing a four-year course in Cranio-Sacral Therapy (CST), which perfectly balances bodywork and therapy together. It works on the spine and the head, but it works through on the whole system. I've started my own practice and, soon, I hope to be able to make a living of it.

So, in the end, I want to use my own experiences to help other people. I'm working with complementary or, alternative medicine, often marginalized as a pseudo science. For me, it worked though and I don't have any doubts about the great potential it has. Just like with mainstream music, there is an alternative to mainstream medicine, as well. Everyone has to follow his or her own path and this is mine. What I want to share in this story is that is okay to ask for help. Talk about your problems and if needed chose a therapist who you trust and takes you as you are. Be your real self, don't suppress feelings, and don't obey authority. Society might call you crazy, to me it is punk!

If you have any comments or questions, feel free to contact me at jaggedvisionszine@gmail.com

bright to a third eye

Anonymous

Today was hard. I tore myself to pieces, again, inside my head. But I have a show on the horizon. Maybe it's in someone's house, maybe it's at a bar. Maybe it's far away. It doesn't matter. I'm in pieces. Soon I'll feel whole again, for a little while. I know this. I feel shitty, but I have something to anticipate. Who knows what will happen or whom I'll talk to there? If I can swing it, I can keep the chill off my heart. I'm grateful as long as I can keep the chill away. I am hoping I learned something from the last time I stumbled hard into depression. I remember the symptom recognition lessons we talked about in the partial-hospital day program, the tiny things I can do against the towering assault of sadness.

I'm there at the show. There are people. There's a pleasant din, shady basement lights, dim bar lights, liquors lifted to kiss their owners. The bands come, they play, and we warm to the energy we make. We laugh and dance. We give each other real hugs. I stand in the shadows and enjoy the milieu. We come here to make our own world—made out of our inexpensive fun, our talent, and our love. We make our own culture. I can feel the love and it's the kind of friendship the norms can only dream of. I can breathe deep again.

I'm smiling. Earlier today, I didn't think I could smile like this. My rational side typically jumps in to protect me, but sometimes it needs to be folded into a hug and eased into true safety against uncertain terrors. I'm smiling hard from deep inside. The dark corners of my very life are pushed up into the light. I can't help this feeling. I'm quenched. I'm pushed to do more. Perhaps, I'm not so horrible after all. People come up to me and say hello, visibly happy to see me. My confidence blooms. There is no substitute for this.

I'm me. In this place, with this noise, with these people, I am closer to me than I can ever be. I am grounded. Life is hyper-real and it doesn't scare me. The noise slams hard into my earplugs and it holds me fast to now and to ME. I look around the room and I realize that I'm proud to know these people. How lucky I am to know these people and feel good about making music for these people.

I look at the faces. I try to imagine what they were like as kids—when they felt scared or sad or confused, when they too felt that they weren't like the other kids in school. I try to imagine them in their hometowns, in their bedrooms, in detention, at shows back in the day. I might know snatches of stories here and there. This person makes jokes about their drunk dad. That person references the years they spent in foster care. Another person over there had good grades and a college education and a cool mom. Another hopped trains or, at least, pretends they did. And, maybe, you've been in six bands since you were thirteen, but none will match the one you had a couple of fierce years ago. Then, I squint my eyes and wonder where we'll be in five or ten or twenty years. Will I be surprised to see the photos that someone is taking right this moment? Will I be surprised by how young we look? Will we remember how crazy we were, or how much better we've been? Years are short, but days are long.

I can only cast this group of people roughly as family, as something I learn about, gradually, in this alternate reality. Punk is rehab; it's vitamins; it's nourishment for our minds and hearts. To quote one of the many songwriters I am privileged to call a friend, it's a match struck against the black. It's a chain that grows, its tendrils wrapped into neighborhoods across cities and states. I meet punks from near and far and the glow remains the same. I smile for that glow from deep down and clear to my face.

Every day, I deal with the legacy of my mental illness. I wake. I work. I play. I sleep. I string together moments. Moments are all we truly have against the backdrop of remembering the past and conjuring the future. When it's bad, my moments throw me. At my worst, I become numb to what I hold dear and I am lost, floundering and drifting into the doldrums of dark memory. But, like the deity I was promised in parochial days, punk is bigger than me, even though, it fits neatly into my heart. It throws stones at my window when I'm hidden in my room. It reaches through a chorus to scratch my head. It smiles at me through a crowd and coaxes me out again. It is unconditional and patient.

Relentlessly, punk taught me to believe in myself and to make my own destiny. In turn, I believe in us punks, too. It's crucial. In order to function, I need to believe that this difficult life is not a waste. Life is because of the points of light that illuminate my night. It's because of whom I saw and chatted with. It's for whom I played and with whom I played. Life is for those who danced for the first time or the millionth time. It's for the thrill I felt, welling up in swells of happiness.

I'm home. I'm pumped. I'm high, thanks to the forty I drank, weed I smoked, and the words I yelled. It's 2:30 in the morning, and I'm praying that my roommates don't wake up because I'm playing along to my band's most recent release and enjoying the fuck out of it. My heart is pumping and I feel deliciously defiant. There are always good days and bad—a constant drizzle over time that must be confronted. Punks, unflinchingly, see the horrors of life. The bottom line in punk is to avoid the unexamined life. We wear the ache of the world scrawled across our bodies and minds. But, because we see the mess, we also see the pleasures and the deep raw ore of creative, outspoken joy. This is perspective. We dare. We fucking dare to find it. We learn to ask the right questions, in order, to examine life. We aspire to burn down the woodwork of the zeitgeist while toasting marshmallows over the embers. For someone who has felt broken for their entire life, like myself, to be encouraged in the hard beauty found in recovery is a gift, like no other. And, punk gets that shit; unconditionally, patiently, persistently.

Because punk is made by what I put into it, what I can put into it, and what I get out of it, it's me. It's me, which is a profound lesson for a person who has brittleness about their soul. It connects me when I feel doomed and damned. I believe it. Punk is the only thing that proves to me that humanity is not completely fucked—punk stares this fuckedness right in the face, like Coyote, the ambiguous trickster who sneaks to turn the page. It's like in dialectical behavioral therapy: you learn to handle bad times just by noticing them honestly and building from there. Counterintuitive at first, but the counterintuitive side of life is where we eagles dare. Punk is the only place where I believe I am not completely fucked and destroyed even though I loudly acknowledge that reality. Punk stands bright to my third eye and I feel the strength of it. What appears to be tatters and darkness is a sign of honesty and comfort, even love.

And I'm still smiling.

Punk Rock Lockdown

Anonymous

Note: in parts of this article, I use the term "patient" to refer to people who are in psychiatric hospitals for treatment of their illness. I realize this term has connotations of nurses, doctors, therapists, psychologists, and social workers (staff) having power over somebody who has things "done to" them (the patient). Given the way that the institution often drives people into accepting certain roles, it seemed to be the best term to use.

For almost three years, I worked as a registered creative psychotherapist, in a secure hospital, for adults with complex and enduring mental health needs. It was tough. I was treating people who were seriously mentally ill—actively psychotic, with unpredictable, and sometimes violent tendencies.

Every patient, in that hospital, was there because he or she had been committed for assessment or treatment under the Mental Health Act. We have laws in the UK which say that if somebody's mental illness is causing them to be a danger to themselves or others, they can be forcibly committed to a secure hospital to be treated. Our NHS system means that nobody goes without treatment for want of health insurance; if you are seriously ill, you will get treatment, whether you like it or not.

In some respects, the law makes sense. People can be violent when they're psychotic. Not everybody who has a mental illness is dangerous—many never hurt anyone—but our patients were. Many had threatened or injured people they loved, or themselves. A lot found their psychotic episodes distressing, to say the least. They believed things that weren't true, and saw and heard things that weren't real. I saw patients who believed they were at the center of a huge persecutory conspiracy, and others who thought their neighbors were plotting to kill them. When people are psychotic, their ability to look after themselves can deteriorate rapidly. I'm not talking about people forgetting to have to bathe every now and again. I'm talking about people who can't eat because of their depression, or who get too paranoid to drink the water coming out of their own taps; people who come dangerously close to dehydration and starvation.

Often, the "treatment" prescribed, within the letter of the law, basically means getting sent to a locked hospital until anti-psychotic medications are started or restarted, and until they start having an effect. This was the sort of hospital in which I worked. When I started there, I had been a registered therapist for about one year, and a punk for about nine.

My first few days there were a real eye opener. Naively, perhaps, I had imagined a place where patients were treated with respect and nurses who had taken up a caring role for the best possible ethical reasons. Instead, I heard nursing assistants joking about "jabbing" (with injected sedatives) patients who gave them any bother and ward managers who tried to stop patients from seeing their families and having access to their own property.

The imbalance of power in these sorts of institutions can be massive. The staff tell the patients when to get up, what to eat and when, and when and where they can go out. In a hospital that has a poor or old-fashioned culture, patients don't always have a lot of say. That's anathema to a punk rocker who is used to making their own rules, or, at least, having a bit of a say in how the rules are made.

It was a shock to find creative therapeutic approaches—like art and music therapy groups—being heavily obstructed by the ward managers. This was often done under the guise of "risk management." There were too many risks inherent, they often said, in bringing equipment onto the ward that patients could use to hurt themselves or others. Yet, patients were given few other opportunities to be creative. No pens or pencils were allowed for unsupervised use, and on the admission ward, patients weren't allowed to have access to their own guitars. I found that pretty inhumane. It was good for patients to have therapeutic conversations with the staff, but not all the staff were conscientious enough to bother, and most days there was nothing for the patients to do. Many spent all day either out in the smoking yard or plonked in front of the TV (again, something I, as a punk rocker, found horrific).

In discussion with other therapists working there, I came to realize that it wasn't the equipment used for art and music therapy groups that managers were scared of at all. It was what therapy *represented*: the idea that dangerous men could be allowed an hour every week to express themselves—during which they were rarely told what to do—where nobody controlled them. That, for many of the staff who had old-fashioned ideas about psychiatric care, was terrifying.

As a punk rocker, my ideals were similar to those I had as a therapist. I wanted people coming to group therapy sessions to be able to use their creativity to escape the drudgery of the ward, for an hour. Playing music, drawing pictures, having a genuine conversation, could take them away from the claustrophobia of the locked doors and the rigid timetables. From my many experiences in the punk rock community, I knew well how creativity can be freeing for anybody . . . even if that creativity goes into working out what meal you can make from a bizarre combination of skipped food.

In the group, attendees could find ways of connecting with one another while still remaining individuals. This is something we do all the time in the punk rock community. We support other people to be themselves, and they support us to be us. We're part of a community, but we will never give up our individuality. Attendees were given the chance to decide how to use their own creativity, a kind of self-determination that wasn't available in ordinary days on the ward. I sought to foster a group culture, in which, every attendee was welcomed for who he or she was, respected as an individual, and supported by the rest of the group. These ideas about how group therapy should work were fostered by my experiences within the DIY community.

Many of my colleagues did not seem to think the patients were capable of thinking about group and community; rather than realizing the patients could think for themselves, many of the nurses were fond of constantly telling the patients what to do. I, often, found that my background as a punk made me more accepting than some of my colleagues. It seemed as though many of the nurses—even the good ones—had become so blinkered by the rigidity of the institution that it started to affect their own thinking.

They would go around the bedrooms mindlessly every morning, getting everyone up so that all of the patients could have breakfast when it was served. Patients were expected to eat what was provided, rather than having any say in their own diet. If anybody deviated from the norm, it could be written up in their notes as evidence of their illness. Once, I heard a nurse talking about a patient who was vegan as being someone who had "delusional ideas about food." There was no consideration, even for a second, that this person might have chosen to avoid animal products for good ethical reasons! It was all too easy for the nurses to get sucked into this "staff-patient" dynamic that made them want to control people's options, almost without thinking. I often felt that, as a punk, I had a wider, more accepting stance about what a reasonable request might be, than somebody who wasn't.

That's not to say that I didn't see any good work while I was there. Many of the nurses, not necessarily punks, fought for the patients to be seen and accepted as individuals. It's good clinical practice to listen respectfully to the people you're treating, and make sure they have a say in their own treatment. But in a place where everything was dictated by risk management and institutional rigidity, persuading the other staff to think humanely was always a bit of a struggle.

During the time I worked there, alongside the permanent low-level anxiety that I might one day be hit or attacked by a patient (always a possibility—although luckily it never happened), I always worried that somebody I knew would be admitted. From listening to gossip, I knew of at least two people who had psychotic illnesses, managed by medication, who weren't "out" about being mentally ill. I worried that, if one of these friends came in, there might be a thought in their head that their secret would be out—that once somebody from the DIY world knew for sure about their illness, that it would be all over the place. Of course, it wouldn't—you'd never discuss something you'd seen at work out of work. All the same, the thought would be there, causing stress and anxiety, potentially delaying recovery for somebody I knew and cared about. It never happened, thankfully, and I was glad that, during those three years, my friends were well enough to stay out of hospital.

Working with people with complex mental health difficulties sometimes sat uneasily against my DIY ideals. A lot of the people I treated had, unsuccessfully, tried to manage their own illnesses in the community. I believed then—and still do now—that there are certain illnesses which need specialized treatment by trained professionals. That might not necessarily mean hospitalization. It might mean a program or therapy and support in the community provided by a specialist team. No matter how well-meaning a group of friends might be, there are some illnesses that will always need, at least, a little professional help. It's important that those doing the "treating" have the training to know what they're doing as well as having good ethics and a commitment to respectful patient care. Without it, the "care" they give might be unhealthy, unhelpful, or worse—dangerous.

I stopped working in the hospital about five years ago. Secure hospitals have something of a life of their own: everything is locked, and everyone—staff and patients—exist in a state of unrelenting stress and anxiety. It was exhausting to, continually, throw myself at the brick wall of an institution that sought to restrict individuality, freedom of thought . . . freedom, full stop! All the same, I feel good that for the time I was there, the patients had access to creative therapy. One of the people I treated once told me, "nobody else in here listens." It wasn't just my therapy training that allowed me to do it, it was my experiences, as a punk. It was knowing that people, even when ill, can be empowered to do something for themselves through genuine experiences, rather than being "told" what to do by a rigid, unmoving establishment.

It saddens me to think that, apart from snide jokes about certain members of our punk rock community being "unbalanced" or "mental," mental health isn't something we talk about. We all know how to support somebody through a break up or traumatic house move, but we don't know how to offer somebody support when they have a chronic mental illness. People feel they can't tell anyone about what they're going through, and some of them feel like they're struggling alone. That is something that needs to change—and I hope it will, someday soon.

A letter from the editor

Dear Reader,

I am a person in recovery from a lifetime of mental health struggle, substance use, and trauma. I have been part of the punk scene since I first discovered it in 1988 and I am now forty years old. I spent my teenage years living in group homes and psychiatric hospitals. For the majority of my adult life, I lived in substandard housing, surrounded by drugs, and, often, by other dysfunctional people. I struggled to maintain employment and I was often indigent. I had difficulty in managing my relationships with others and often experienced alienation and interpersonal conflict with my peers. I lived this unhappy and unsatisfying life, for years on end, until I was able to begin to take steps to improve the quality of my life.

In the mid 2000s, I hit rock bottom and seriously considered taking my own life. I instead sought out therapy and began meeting with a wonderful therapist on a regular basis. This therapist validated me and my experiences and I was able to begin to pull myself up out of the gutter that I had, perpetually, lived in. I was able to continue to take positive steps forward and my quality of life was improving. The road ahead was frightening, yet, I persevered and fought, as hard as I could, to create a life of wellness and stability for myself.

Currently, I work as a peer mental health counselor at a human services agency in Boston. I have kept this job for over four years, which, is the longest I have ever kept a job. I have also authored a book titled *Better Days: A Mental Health Recovery Workbook*, which is based on my personal struggle to create a better life for myself. This book has been well received and I am having a lot of fun giving workshops, presentations, and communicating with people all over the world.

More recently, I have been travelling to different cities throughout the United States and Canada telling the story of my life, much like the writers in this book have told their stories. It is personally important to me to share what I have experienced in life, with my peers, because I want people to know that life can, indeed, become better and that there are things we can do to create happier and healthier lives for ourselves. I will not allow my suffering to be wasted. Oi! Oi! Oi!

Sincerely,
Crusty Craig
February 13, 2014

Better Days Recovery Press has also published the 'Better Days - A Mental Health Recovery Workbook' written by Craig Lewis

This book helps those aspiring toward recovery and also those in recovery, because it addresses and challenges the individual—in very real, basic and honest ways—to make significant cognitive adjustments in how they live their lives. The beauty of this curriculum is that people want to do it and don't consider it a chore, a demand, or a requirement, because every page subtlely encourages the individual to think in realistic and forward-moving ways. This allows them to feel good about doing the work.

I based this book on my personal life and recovery, and every page has been used successfully in peer group settings.

Craig Lewis is a Certified Peer Specialist living and working in Massachusetts. He has struggled immensely with mental health issues throughout his life, but he has successfully transformed this into a life of wellness. He has embraced his recovery process, producing remarkably beneficial results. He has discovered that he has innate skills and capabilities for helping others in their recovery, and he has been able to help many people improve the quality of their lives, which is life-affirming for him. He does this by tapping into his lived experience to help others transcend their own struggles. He is sincerely committed to his recovery and helping nurture the recovery and wellness of all with whom he comes into contact. Craig is successfully working as part of an outreach team at a human services agency in Boston, Massachusetts. He also tours the country, speaking about his lived experience, sharing his struggles and triumphs to help others.

WWW.BETTERDAYSRECOVERY.COM